# WHY AM I HERE?

## The soul, the Guru and the path

## TARSEM SINGH

**Foreword by Raman Singh**
**Founder of the Sikhi Enlightenment Course**

# TABLE OF CONTENTS

# PREFACE

The purpose of life is a search for more than temporary happiness. When you dive deeply into yourself, a new awakening occurs. This awakening is hidden away because of attachment to the outer, material world and the constant desire towards that which we have not felt, experienced or accomplished in our lives. Once you recognise that you are more than just a body with a short-term identity, the pathway to return to God opens.

> O my mind, you are the embodiment of the Divine Light
> - recognise your own origin.
> *Guru Amar Daas Jee - Sri Guru Granth Sahib Jee - 440*

Realising your true self is more than just a journey. It is a passion, dedication, and a way of life. The human body is equipped to reveal the Divine Light inside you. But you have been born in a dark age, where countless distractions exist to tempt and mislead you. Attachment and desire are the two fixations which have created a wall-like materialistic veil that separates you from God. The good news is that the ever-awake Guru can remove this veil and awaken you.

Only the Guru is awake; the rest of the world is asleep in emotional attachment and desire. Those who serve the True Guru and remain wakeful, are imbued with the True Name, the treasure of virtue.

*Guru Amar Daas Jee - Sri Guru Granth Sahib Jee - 592*

The light of Guru Nanak journeyed through the bodies of ten Gurus and is forever present in the loving words and everlasting Guru called Guru Granth Sahib Jee. The writings are called "Gurbani" and were revealed here on earth for anyone who is seeking their purpose. The poetic writings are truly fascinating with a clear thread running through them about our soul and its relationship with God. They transcend all of the things that divide the human race like social class and inequality. By meeting the Guru and surrendering the ego to the Words of Gurbani, we begin our journey to meet God.

The purpose of this book is two-fold. One is to understand why the mind is so entrenched in an illusion. The second is to inspire you to awaken from this sleep and discover your true self through the universal message of the Guru. Many books explore mainstream practices, whereas this book aims to take a deep dive into the plight of the soul in a way that is accessible to all. To explore how the Guru's wisdom ends pain and suffering and liberates the soul.

You are about to embark on a soul-searching journey that will be transformational and liberating! It will help you form a relationship with your soul. Your whole life could take a very positive turn, so embrace the change and start taking steps towards your destination. You will not regret it!

**Tarsem Singh**

# FOREWORD

While delivering the Sikhi Enlightenment Course throughout the UK and Europe, it became very evident to me that spirituality is often interpreted as a set of rules of what you can and can't do, while not focussing on things that truly matter. Modern preaching about the Sikh faith has also predominantly focussed on the traditions and outer practices, which are undoubtedly important. Still, it often distracts from the essential core spiritual goals of life. This book attempts to steer our focus back to some of these universal topics by exploring the wisdom of the Guru's teachings concisely and clearly. It is difficult to do full justice to such a vast array of knowledge, hence why one of the tasks the book concludes with is to continue your learning journey after reading it.

Often when we think about deep meditation, the first picture that may come to our minds is that of a monk in unique clothes, sitting detached on a mountain or in the forest. We rarely imagine a householder in a living room in a deep meditative state, doing day to day activities just like us. Or going to work and wearing clothes just like we do, but remaining connected to God intuitively. When we think of spiritual scriptures too, we may think of ancient or out-of-date texts that are reserved for those detached monks. Yet comparatively, Gurbani is a very recent gift for mankind that seems to become more and more relevant day by day.

I am really excited that this book is available for all to explore and learn about why we are all here. Like the course, it provides a structured framework for daily life, and a baseline to realign our hopes and desires. I am sure it will appeal to a broad audience, both young and old, regardless of faith and background.


**Raman Singh**
**Founder of the Sikhi Enlightenment Course**
**9th October 2020**

# CHAPTER 1

# Living for a purpose

## Born to be original but dying as a copy

We have come to earth for a reason! We share this planet with many other life forms, but human beings are unusually distinct. We have some extraordinary capabilities compared to the animal kingdom, and our intelligence enables us to have a significant impact on this world. Humans are exceptionally resilient and can survive in the most hostile conditions by adapting to surroundings and devising creative ways to live. We can co-operate flexibly by making decisions on how to live alongside each other and the rest of creation.

We may take our ability to speak, think, care, love, and live a longer life compared to other creatures entirely for granted. Yet these strengths and skills make us the most powerful part of creation. The weakness that we have is that our inner desires are always increasing, and this fascination with the world misdirects us from our purpose.

> Other life forms are your slaves and water-carriers; in this
> world, you are a ruler. Gold, silver and wealth are yours,
> but lustful promiscuity destroys the best of your conduct.
> *Guru Arjan Dev Jee - Sri Guru Granth Sahib Jee – 373*

Our selfish hopes and misdirected desires create divisions and make us weak. Life becomes a competition and a race for more. We create social and political divides that are reactive, destructive and unproductive. Our personal lives become a show for others to admire. The choices we make are driven by external factors, and we live our lives to meet the expectations of others.

> They belong to the human species, but they act like animals.
> Day and night, they live their life just as a show for others.
> *Guru Arjan Dev Jee - Sri Guru Granth Sahib Jee - 267*

When we are driven by selfishness, our instinctive behaviour lowers our capabilities. This animal-like behaviour becomes our nature, which entrenches us deeper into this world of illusion. We learn from the Guru's wisdom that we are very fortunate to have this human body. Our eternal souls have journeyed through many lives to reach this stage. Our human body is the pinnacle of creation, but it is only temporary. We are at the crossroads of either ending this cycle or returning 'into life' over and over again.

> Hate, conflict, sexual desire, anger, emotional attachment,
> falsehood, corruption, immense greed and deceit: So many
> lifetimes have been wasted in these ways. Nanak: uplift the
> mortal, and redeem him, O Lord - show Your Mercy!
> Guru Arjan Dev Jee - Sri Guru Granth Sahib Jee - 267

## My relationship with everything but myself

If we ask ourselves who we are, we can probably answer from

several viewpoints. Sometimes this question seems trivial or even condescending. We may have never viewed this as a problem, so we may not feel the need to answer it

The answer to this question starts to get complicated because we identify with many things. Who we are changes depending on different perspectives, such as family life, professional life and our social life. From a family perspective, we may identify as a relative, such as a mother or a father. From a professional standpoint, our career or job title may give us a form of identity. And if we look at the social or personal perspective, our beliefs or even our hobbies may form a substantial part of our identity. If we step back and evaluate these identities, we realise that they all relate to something external. We are husbands of our partners, mothers of our children, professionals in a career, and members of a group or an association. Even our names were given to us by our family environment. Our changing identities become more evident when we look at our lives through stages. For instance, when we are young, we are regarded as teenagers, then as middle-aged adults, and then as elderly.

What we identify with is determined by our environment, our stage in life and our beliefs. We can spend our lives as just a related part to something temporary without ever searching to understand our true self. It is not hard to understand why, because we spend most of our lives paying attention to the things that are outside. We only focus on our inner world or feelings when there is some form of crisis, like sadness or anger. When we read the spiritual scriptures of Gurbani, the spoken words of the Guru, we begin to understand that the emphasis is very much on an inner journey rather than an outer one.

O human being, search your own heart every day and do not wander around in confusion.

Our soul sits silently in the background, while our mind continually interacts with the body. Yet the soul is timeless, and the body is not. By searching inwards, we awaken our mind to its relationship with the soul. Our worldly connections that shape our identities are temporary and will not be there with us when the soul leaves.

Where there is no mother, father, children, friends or siblings, O my mind, there, only the Naam, the Name of the Lord, shall be with you as your help and support.
*Guru Arjan Dev Jee - Sri Guru Granth Sahib Jee - 264*

All of our relationships with the world will end, and the identities that we have created will no longer be relevant. But what is this soul that moves on after this life and does not die? To answer this question, it helps first to recognise what we are not. There is a beautiful Shabad (a poetic verse) in Gurbani, which helps us answer this difficult question that even experienced spiritual searchers have struggled to comprehend.

It is not human, and it is not a deity. It is not a celibate, or a worshipper of Shiva, the goddess. It is not a Yogi, and it is not a hermit. It is not a mother or anyone's son. ||1|| Then what is it, which dwells in this temple of the body? No one can find the limits to this question. ||1||Pause|| It is not a house-holder, and it is not a renouncer of the world. It is not a king, and it is not a beggar. It has no body, no drop of blood. It is not a Brahmin, and it is not a Khashatri warrior. ||2|| It is not a man of austere self-discipline or a Muslim Sheikh. It does not live, and it is not seen to die. If

someone cries over its death, that person loses their
honour. ||3||
By Guru's Grace, I have found the Path. Birth and death
have both been erased. Says Kabeer, this soul is of the
same essence as the Lord. Like permanent ink becomes
part of the paper which nobody can erase. ||4||2||5||.
*Bhagat Kabeer Jee - Sri Guru Granth Sahib Jee - 871*

Our mind and body may think that we are any one of those things,
but the soul is part of God. Just like a drop of water is part of the
ocean. When everything that we know perishes, it will still not
die. We need to take a moment to stop and contemplate on this.
We have discovered a new identity, which is not only real but also
permanent.

## What is my purpose?

This life is a precious opportunity to achieve much more than
personal accomplishments. Our purpose is far more significant than
heritage, career or even family. Hopes, desires and ambitions all
tend to be very short term because our understanding of happiness
and peace of mind is short-term too. We have a tremendous
opportunity to meet God. To unite again like a droplet of water
merges back with the ocean.

This human body has been given to you. This is your chance
to meet the Lord of the Universe. All other efforts are of
little use to you. Join the Saadh Sangat, the Company of
the Holy; vibrate and meditate on the Jewel of the Naam.
*Guru Arjan Dev Jee - Sri Guru Granth Sahib Jee - 12*

The number of breaths or time that we have to achieve this union
with God is limited. As time passes day by day, each breath is

strengthening temporary foundations. Guru Jee says that our breaths are like jewels that we are trading in for very little return. God is calling for us to return home. Temporary riches and pleasures will never make us truly happy. True happiness comes from experiencing a higher state; one of bliss that leads us back to God.

> The One who sent you has now recalled you; return to your home in peace and harmony. In bliss and ecstasy, sing His Glorious Praises; by this spiritual tune, you shall acquire your everlasting kingdom.
>
> *Guru Arjan Dev Jee - Sri Guru Granth Sahib Jee - 678*

# Questions to think over

How have my family, race, past, and other aspects of life formed my identity?

What have I considered to be my main purpose in life?

Knowing that I originate from God, how does it change my perception of the world?

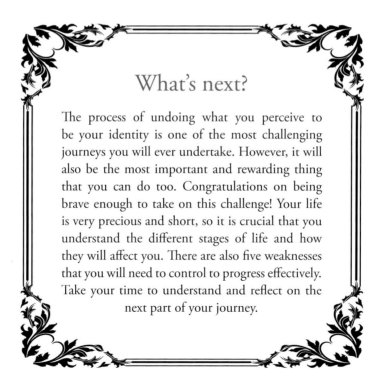

## What's next?

The process of undoing what you perceive to be your identity is one of the most challenging journeys you will ever undertake. However, it will also be the most important and rewarding thing that you can do too. Congratulations on being brave enough to take on this challenge! Your life is very precious and short, so it is crucial that you understand the different stages of life and how they will affect you. There are also five weaknesses that you will need to control to progress effectively. Take your time to understand and reflect on the next part of your journey.

# CHAPTER 2

# Life as a human being

## Coming to this world

Our human journey started in the womb. During those months in the womb, Guru Jee tells us that we had an unbroken bond with God. This perfect connection protected us during this phase. Our lives are described very beautifully as a merchant travelling in four watches of the night. The existence in the womb is the initial phase of life or the first watch of the night. The other three watches are childhood, adulthood and then old age.

> In the first watch of the night, O my merchant friend, the Lord places you in the womb. You meditate on the Lord and chant the Lord's Name, O my merchant friend. You contemplate the Name of the Lord, Har, Har. Chanting the Name, Har, Har, and meditating on it within the fire of the womb, your life was sustained by dwelling on the Naam.
>
> *Guru Raam Daas Jee - Sri Guru Granth Sahib Jee – 76*

Our protection in the womb was our loving bond with God through Naam – the Name of God. When we were born, our connection with God broke away because of our attraction to the world. Our goal in life is to re-establish that love which kept us alive in the womb.

> The loving connection with the Lord wears off, and the child becomes attached to desires; Maya (illusion) exerts its strength.
> *Guru Amar Daas Jee - Sri Guru Granth Sahib Jee – 918*

## Stages of life

There are many distractions which change and develop as we go through the different stages of life. There are ten stages, and at each of these stages, we get consumed by a distraction. Each part of life will make us feel that the world is actual and that God is either far away or does not exist.

| STAGE | ATTRACTION | AGE |
|-------|------------|-----|
| Stage 1 | Love for milk | 0 to 12 |
| Stage 2 | Recognition of mother and father | |
| Stage 3 | Love for brothers and sisters | |

| Stage 4 | Absorbed in games and playing | 13 to 32 |
|---|---|---|
| Stage 5 | Love for eating and drinking | |
| Stage 6 | Distracted by lustful thoughts | |
| Stage 7 | A desire for companionship, marriage and a home | 33 to 62 |
| Stage 8 | Clinging to stubbornness which causes anger | |
| Stage 9 | Overcome by old age | 63+ |
| Stage 10 | The final stage, meeting death | |

In our childhood, we first fall in love with milk, and then we cherish our relationships with our family. As we get older, we immerse ourselves in games and the pleasures of food, drink and lust. Then we settle down into marriage and family life. As the days go by, everything in our past becomes nothing more than a dream. Feelings of unfulfillment, frustration, regret and anger can be strife in later life. The years go by quite quickly, and when we look back on our lives, nothing is tangible anymore. We have our memories, but we have no way of reliving our past. Our reality becomes a dream or memory after each and every passing second, but we do not realise it. Before we know it, it is time to depart.

> At the age of ten, he is a child; at twenty, a youth, and at thirty, he is called handsome. At forty, he is full of life; at fifty, his footing in youth starts to slip away, and at sixty, old age is upon him. At seventy, he loses his intellect, and at eighty, he cannot perform his duties. At ninety, he lies

in his bed, and he cannot understand his weakness. After seeking and searching for such a long time, O Nanak, I have seen that the world is just a mansion of smoke.

*Guru Nanak Dev Jee - Sri Guru Granth Sahib Jee – 138*

## Five internal emotions

There are many different types of emotions that influence how we feel, live and how we interact with others in our life. At times, it may seem like these emotions overtake us. There are five passions in the body which are necessary for our survival but end up driving what we do and how we interrelate. They are lust, anger, greed, attachment and egotistical pride. Gurbani refers to them in different ways such as thieves, weaknesses, evils, fires etc. As we go through the stages of life, these five weaknesses affect us in different ways. When we operate through our ego-driven nature, we do not progress spiritually because our inner positive emotions become suppressed. Guru Jee calls these inner passions 'thieves' because they rob us of our spiritual connection with God.

Within this body dwell the five thieves: sexual desire, anger, greed, emotional attachment and egotistical pride. They plunder the Nectar, but the self-willed manmukh does not realise it; no one hears his complaint. The world is blind, and its dealings are blind as well; without the Guru, there is only pitch darkness.

*Guru Amar Daas Jee - Sri Guru Granth Sahib Jee - 600*

By single-mindedly connecting with God through the Guru's teachings, we produce "Amrit"; the divine inner nectar which enlightens us in this world and is our wealth for the next world.

Amrit elevates us above the mortal world to merge us back with God. Misguided by our senses, we allow the five internal thieves to drive us away from the nectar. When this happens, the mind then feels distant from God. The five evils are fighters, and the battle takes place in the body. It requires the strength of a warrior and the qualities of a saint to beat them. Just as there are five adverse passions, there are five Godly ones too. These five allow for the inner nectar to grow and prosper.

> Truth, contentment, compassion, faith and purity - I have received the Teachings that ignite these from the Saints.
> *Guru Arjan Dev Jee - Sri Guru Granth Sahib Jee - 822*

There are many negative energies interconnected with the five passions. Together, they form a powerful illusion called "Maya" that makes us think that they are permanent when they are not. We need to rid ourselves of everything that is causing turmoil in our lives to be absorbed in God. One fascinating Shabad summarises this by guiding us on what we need to remove.

> Renounce lust, anger, falsehood and slander; forsake Maya and eliminate egotistical pride. Renounce sexual desire and promiscuity, and give up emotional attachment. Only then shall you obtain the Immaculate Lord amidst the darkness of the world. Renounce selfishness, conceit and arrogant pride, and your love for your children and spouse. Abandon your thirsty hopes and desires and remain connected with the Lord. O Nanak, the True One shall come to dwell in your mind. Through the True Word of the Shabad, you shall be absorbed in the Name of the Lord.
> *Guru Raam Daas Jee - Sri Guru Granth Sahib Jee - 141*

As human beings, we face a significant challenge to remove

ingrained habits that may have been with us for lifetimes. The Words of the Guru's Shabads are here to help us with this challenge. By keeping these words enshrined in our hearts, we can abandon our weaknesses and realise our real personality and character.

# Questions to think over

What stage of life am I at now, and what effect is that stage having on me?

How have my senses restricted my understanding of the world around me?

How prominent are the five weaknesses in my life?

## What's next?

You will hopefully have a better understanding of what stage you are in your life and how five evils affect you in our day to day activities. It takes a true warrior to fight these forces, so well done and keep persevering! You have done well to get to this stage. You will now get to learn about what is driving you and how the external world is influencing you. By understanding the Guru's message, you will be able to transform your drivers into helpful ones. You will also learn about values and why the right ones are essential in spiritual life.

# CHAPTER 3

# What is driving our lives?

### The influences around you

The world is continually changing, so keeping up to date with what is happening around us is essential. Today, the primary sources for information are the television, smartphone and the internet, and it may come as no surprise that using technology has become our main spare-time activity. Not so long ago, the television business was broadcaster driven. There were limited channels, and viewers could select from a handful of channels. The whole industry has now changed to being consumer-driven, where viewers now decide what they watch and when. Digital recorders are now pushing content to us based on what they predict we will like. Binge-watching, watching media for long periods without control, is now all too common thanks to platforms like Youtube and other web media and television sites.

What we watch will no doubt influence us in many important ways. Our views on the environment, politics, health and even body image, could be shaped by what we consume digitally. The whole picture gets more complicated when we combine our life experiences into the equation. Our needs, emotions and our family and friends drive what we do too.

We form a set of values based on all these complex influences. These values can be both positive or negative. Examples of negative values are a belief that violence solves problems or that racism can be justified. People can be very cold and even evil to others. Values can actually drive you away from God too. If our values are not bringing us closer to God, then we need to question ourselves on how we have reached this stage.

> O mind, what evil-mindedness have you developed? You are engrossed in the pleasures of other men's wives, and slander; yet you have not worshipped the Lord at all.
> *Guru Tegh Bahadur Jee - Sri Guru Granth Sahib Jee - 631*

If meeting God is not at the forefront of our lives, then our efforts may fulfil a short-term need, but they will not genuinely benefit us, or the world around us.

> Making all sorts of efforts, they wander around; but they do not make even one fruitful effort. O Nanak, how rare are those who understand the effort which saves the whole world.
> *Guru Nanak Dev Jee - Sri Guru Granth Sahib Jee – 965*

## The drive for more

If achieving fame and accumulating wealth was the key to happiness, then all of the celebrities that we see would be living a joyous life. In many cases, nothing could be further from the truth. Sometimes they live their life under a microscope, and they attract fake friends. It is not uncommon to see that they are suffering from mental health issues. The media also plays a very destructive role in their lives, and often their sorrow is revealed to us very openly.

In some cases, their distresses and misfortune have led them to a tragic end. The reality is that the more we acquire, the more pain we bring upon ourselves. A wealthy person is always in fear of losing what they have. The mind's desire for attaining more never ends too.

> The rulers of all the world are unhappy; one who chants the Name of the Lord becomes happy. By acquiring hundreds of thousands and millions, desires shall not be contained. Chanting the Name of the Lord, you shall find release.
> *Guru Arjan Dev Jee - Sri Guru Granth Sahib Jee - 264*

As we achieve worldly success in life, our expectations and desires also increase. As a result, we are never content, and we only have short spells of happiness. Our sensory organs are never satisfied and always want more. We cannot rely on them to guide us on what is essential for us.

> The mouth is not satisfied by speaking, and the ears are not contented by hearing. The eyes are not fulfilled by seeing; each organ absorbs itself in one sensory quality.
> *Guru Angad Dev Jee - Sri Guru Granth Sahib Jee - 147*

The more we have, the more we will want. Money, power and lust are like fires, the more you feed them, the bigger they get. If we genuinely want to find contentment, our obsession with such materialistic possessions needs to stop. There is nothing wrong with appreciating a promising career or wanting the best for your family. But this should not be at the core of what makes us who we are. Our love and sincerity to God are what we should value from our heart.

> The Lord is my Love; the Lord is my way of life; the Lord is my speech and conversation. By Guru's Grace, my mind is saturated with the Lord's Love; this is what makes up my service.
>
> *Guru Amar Daas Jee - Sri Guru Granth Sahib Jee - 490*

## Giving life meaning

Whenever we ask for happiness, it will always come with its own associated pain. Pleasure and pain are a package. We can never experience constant happiness through material things because everything physical must come to an end.

> O Nanak, it is absurd to ask to be spared from pain by begging for comfort. Pleasure and pain are the two garments that people wear, given by the Court of the Lord.
>
> *Guru Nanak Dev Jee - Sri Guru Granth Sahib Jee - 149*

We will undoubtedly receive some form of pain in our lives. How we handle that pain is our choice. We can either suffer and agonise in pain or, we can learn from it and treat it like a blessing. If we want to find true happiness, then we must go through pain. Think of it like medicine, which does not taste very good, but it is for our benefit. We all want happiness, but that joy can be a disease if it only makes us forget God.

> Suffering is the medicine, and pleasure the disease because where there is pleasure, there is no desire for God.
>
> *Guru Nanak Dev Jee - Sri Guru Granth Sahib Jee - 469*

Our lives will never feel truly meaningful if our drive is limited to our small, self-centred world. Living a life that is inspired by the Guru is true freedom. It leads us to self-realisation and connection with the whole universe. We can build resilience to tolerate sadness and rise above it. In this state, there is no want for joy or avoidance of sorrow. There is also not thirst for praise or fear of losing. Remembering our higher purpose is the key to giving meaning to our lives.

> That mortal, who in the midst of pain, does not feel pain, who is not affected by pleasure, affection or fear, and who looks alike upon gold and dust; Who is not swayed by either slander or praise, nor affected by greed, attachment or pride; who remains unaffected by joy and sorrow, honour and dishonour; who renounces all hopes and desires and remains desire-less in the world; who is not touched by sexual desire or anger - within their heart, God dwells. That mortal, blessed by Guru's Grace, understands this way. O Nanak, they merge with the Lord of the Universe, like water with water.
>
> *Guru Tegh Bahadur Jee - Sri Guru Granth Sahib Jee - 633*

In life, accumulating less and having fewer obligations gives you more time to focus on what is essential. Our inner battle becomes a conscious one with a clear set of drivers that lead to a higher state of consciousness.

> Those things, which caused me such anxiety, have all vanished. Now, I sleep in peace and tranquillity, and my mind is in a state of deep and profound peace; the inverted lotus of my heart has blossomed forth. Behold, a wondrous miracle has happened! That Lord and Master, whose wisdom is said to be unfathomable, has been enshrined within my heart, by the Guru. The demons which tormented me so

much, have themselves become terrified. They pray: please, save us from your Lord Master; we seek your protection.

*Guru Arjan Dev Jee - Sri Guru Granth Sahib Jee - 612*

# Questions to think over

What do I value in life the most? Am I loyal to my values?

Which people and what influences have impacted my life the most? What would my friends say is my primary driver?

What are my spiritual drivers?

How do I handle pain in my life? How can I rise above it?

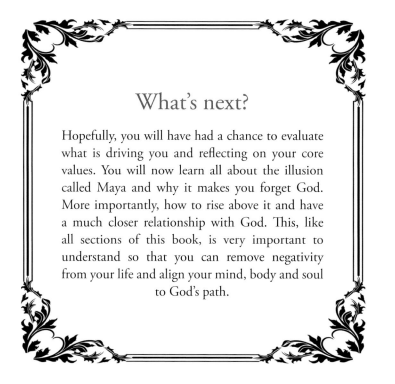

## What's next?

Hopefully, you will have had a chance to evaluate what is driving you and reflecting on your core values. You will now learn all about the illusion called Maya and why it makes you forget God. More importantly, how to rise above it and have a much closer relationship with God. This, like all sections of this book, is very important to understand so that you can remove negativity from your life and align your mind, body and soul to God's path.

# CHAPTER 4

# You reap what you sow

## Is my destiny already written?

Nothing happens by chance - everything happens for a reason. We reap in the future what we have sown in the past.

> You shall harvest what you plant. O Nanak, by the Hukam of God's Command, we come and go in reincarnation.
> *Guru Nanak Dev Jee - Sri Guru Granth Sahib Jee - 4*

Every thought we have, every word we speak and every action we take will affect us in some way, shape or form. Who we are today and the environment that we exist in is all a result of our past. How we respond to our circumstances shapes our destiny. This cycle is the "law of Karam" (popularly known as karma) which is a divine law occurring in God's Will.

> As is the Hukam of Your Command, so do things happen. Wherever You keep me, it is there that I remain and stand.
> *Guru Arjan Dev Jee - Sri Guru Granth Sahib Jee - 633*

# Good and bad actions

When we allow our Godly qualities to guide us, we progress quickly in reaching our destination. Alternatively, when we act selfishly through our vices, we bring about adverse consequences which result in pain and suffering. We are like boats, trying to cross over an ocean. Every adverse action puts a hole at the bottom of our vessel. A light boat with small holes can still reach the shore, whereas one that has a heavy load with large holes will sink.

> Kabeer, the boat is old, and it has thousands of holes. Those who are light get across. While those who carry the weight of their sins on their heads are drowned.
> *Bhagat Kabeer Jee - Sri Guru Granth Sahib Jee - 1366*

Spiritual wealth accumulates within us to help us to complete our journey across the ocean of life. This wealth will help us by repairing our boat, reducing the burden we have accumulated, and further preventing us from adding more adverse weight. Enlightenment happens when we do good, live righteously and break away our bonds with the world.

> Those contented beings serve and meditate on the Truest of the True. They do not place their feet in sin, but do good deeds and live righteously. They burn away the bonds of the world and eat a simple diet of grain and water. You are the Great Forgiver; You give continually, more and more each day. By worshipping His greatness, the Great Lord is obtained.
> *Guru Nanak Dev Jee - Sri Guru Granth Sahib Jee - 466*

The Guru' Shabads are an incredible gift that can erase lifetimes of adverse actions that have been accumulated. By slowly stilling the mind through the Words of the Guru, the inner cleansing happens swiftly and almost miraculously.

> The Word of the Guru's Shabad eradicates the karma of millions of past actions.
>
> *Ramanand Jee - Sri Guru Granth Sahib Jee - 1195*

Through the Guru's teachings, we realise that we have come to this world with more than what is visible to us. Our past actions can be favourable or unfavourable. Guru Jee tells us that even though we may have developed virtues, they should not be taken for granted because we can lose them through our ignorance.

> In your mind, you do not remember the One Lord-you fool! You have forgotten the Lord; your virtues shall wither away.
>
> *Guru Nanak Dev Jee - Sri Guru Granth Sahib Jee - 12*

## Maya – the illusion and it's three modes

When we forget God and become attached to something temporary, we are in a state of duality; the confusion that the creation is permanent and our place in it is too. This state is called "Maya".

> This is Maya, by which the Lord is forgotten; emotional attachment wells up, and duality is loved. Says Nanak, by Guru's Grace, those who enshrine love for the Lord find Him, in the midst of Maya.
>
> *Guru Nanak Dev Jee - Sri Guru Granth Sahib Jee - 12*

Guru Jee says that Maya has spread its net across the whole world. We fall in love with things that stimulate our senses, give us comfort or some form of recognition. In Maya, love for God is exchanged for attachment to the world and the sensual pleasures of the body.

> Emotional attachment to Maya is spread out all over the world. Seeing a beautiful woman, the man is overcome with sexual desire. His love for his children and gold steadily increases. He sees everything as his own but makes the One Lord an outsider. *Guru Nanak Dev Jee - Sri Guru Granth Sahib Jee - 1342*

Maya has three modes, and by forgetting God, we perform our actions across these modes. When we behave with our base, animalistic nature, then we are said to be in "Tamo". A perceived threat to our life, our possessions or our reputation can drop us into Tamo. They are animal-like because different parts of creation also have similar instincts for survival. These instincts are triggered by the physical body and not the soul. Anger, fear, lust and selfishness are all examples of our lower-self.

> Hate, conflict, sexual desire, anger, emotional attachment, falsehood, corruption, immense greed and deceit: So many lifetimes are wasted in these ways. Nanak: uplift them, and redeem them, O Lord - show Your Mercy! *Guru Arjan Dev Jee - Sri Guru Granth Sahib Jee - 267*

The desire for pleasures, fame, acknowledgement and recognition takes us into the second mode called "Rajo". Lust and greed, when uncontrolled, are never satisfied and make us feel that we need more and more. We want a status that is seen and valued. When we experience these things, we do not want to go back. If we lose them, then the desire to get them back increases. These are forceful drivers that can take over our whole outlook on life.

Your home, power and wealth will be of no use to you. Your corrupt worldly entanglements will be of no use to you. Know that all your dear friends are false. Only the Name of the Lord, Har, Har, will go along with you.

*Guru Arjan Dev Jee - Sri Guru Granth Sahib Jee - 889*

When we rise above these two states and try to do good, we are said to be in the mode of "Sato". Sato is a mode where virtues are more prominent. Although we do good, we do it for some form of recognition or reward. Guru Jee teaches us that a desire for salvation or heaven is also Maya. We could have a virtuous character, but it does not mean our ego has subdued.

The righteous do righteous deeds but waste them by asking for the doorway to salvation.

*Guru Nanak Dev Jee - Sri Guru Granth Sahib Jee - 468*

All three of these modes are Maya because they make us forget God, lead to emotional attachment and the love for duality. We must rise above these three states and reach the fourth state called "Turiya". When our actions are performed to merge the soul while being absorbed in the love of God, they are then above the three states.

The world is in the grip of the three qualities; only a few attain the fourth state of absorption. O Nanak, the Saints, are pure and immaculate; the Lord abides within their minds.

*Guru Arjan Dev Jee - Sri Guru Granth Sahib Jee - 297*

How we behave and how we make others act around us has a lasting effect on us. We have accumulated a lot of baggage during our journey, but now it is time to let that baggage go. Our actions control our destiny, so we need to ensure that we are not only doing the right things but also doing them for the right reasons and thinking in the right way too.

# Questions to think over

What am I doing that is creating a burden for me in my life?

What can I do to "lighten the load" and stay focussed on my purpose?

What actions am I doing in the states of "Tamo", "Rajo" and "Sato"?

Is there anything I am doing that is causing others to go into the state of Tamo?

Do I seek reward when I do good or something spiritual?

What am I doing in my life that is connecting my soul with God?

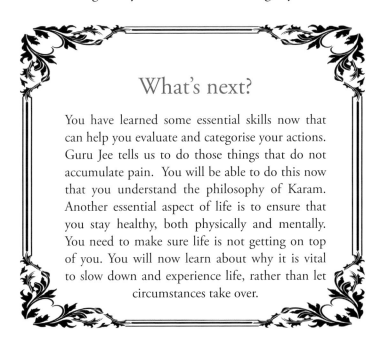

## What's next?

You have learned some essential skills now that can help you evaluate and categorise your actions. Guru Jee tells us to do those things that do not accumulate pain. You will be able to do this now that you understand the philosophy of Karam. Another essential aspect of life is to ensure that you stay healthy, both physically and mentally. You need to make sure life is not getting on top of you. You will now learn about why it is vital to slow down and experience life, rather than let circumstances take over.

# CHAPTER 5

# Slow down and let go

## The mind in overdrive

There is intense and growing pressure to go out more, acquire more, and be more. This pressure comes from external influences, like advertising and social media or internally from our values and thought process. The mind is either racing with thoughts of the future or cycling through events of the past. This constant thinking makes it very ill-prepared to handle the challenges that it will face today.

Technology has also impacted our lives in many ways. We are continually bombarded with dangers, what is good or bad for us, what we should be buying, how we should look and all sorts of other information. Tweeting, texting, messaging, favourites, videos and photos have overtaken our lives. We now have two modes; a real-world and a virtual profile. Our reality is so far away from our ideals that we have to put on a show of happiness. Businesses and corporations are cashing in on the chaos because their product sales and profits depend on our need for them. But spending more does not seem to make us happier. We can spend a lot of time dwelling on what we think we need, rather than be grateful for what we already have. Again, hopes and desires come to the forefront of our lives.

We have very few filters to absorb only that which is necessary. All of this disorder is having a detrimental effect on our physical and mental health. We may become more prone to psychological issues such as anxiety, depression, and loneliness. Or, we may just be setting unrealistic expectations which lead to jealousy, hate and resentment. Social media is also the cause or contributor to breakdowns in family and social relationships.

Time is very precious, yet it feels as though everything is too fast, and we are not productive. Day by day, we are building up our personal stories. We make choices, take individual paths to build up those stories. We should be savouring our present and setting up our future. We can only do this consciously and slowly.

> Involved in worldly affairs, he wastes his life in vain; the peace-giving Lord does not come to abide in his mind.
> *Guru Amar Daas Jee - Sri Guru Granth Sahib Jee - 643*

## Awareness of mental health

Our hectic lifestyles are having a detrimental effect on our mental health. In 2014, the Mental Health Association from the UK published figures in the Adult Psychiatric Morbidity Survey (APMS). They highlighted that every week, one in six adults experiences symptoms of a common mental health problem, such as anxiety or depression. One in five adults has considered taking their own life at some point. Nearly half of all adults believe that, in their lifetime, they have had a diagnosable mental health problem. Yet, only a third have received a diagnosis.

Women between the ages of 16 and 24 are almost three times as likely (at 26%) to experience a common mental health problem as their male contemporaries (9%). They have higher rates of self-harm, bipolar disorder and post-traumatic stress disorder. Another group at particular risk includes people between the ages of 55 and 64. Further, they reported very worrying levels of poor mental health among people receiving Employment and Support Allowance. Two-thirds say they have common mental health problems and the same percentage report suicidal thoughts. 43.2% having made a suicide attempt and one third (33.5%) self-harming.

One certainty in life is that we will experience both ups and downs. Things are always changing, and life brings about many challenges which in turn can lead to pain, suffering and disorder. Those who handle ups and downs in a balanced way through calmness and stability come through healthily. A good or bad event in life should not define us or overturn our balanced mental state. It is just a small segment of a more significant journey. By slowing down, we come to recognise this and take control of our circumstances. Maya is an illusion that torments us when we allow ourselves to drown in the waves of these ups and downs.

> It torments those who act, entangled in ego. It torments us through household affairs, and it troubles us in renunciation. It torments us through character, lifestyle and social status. It torments us through everything that we do, except for those who remain imbued with the Love of the Lord.
>
> *Guru Arjan Dev Jee - Sri Guru Granth Sahib Jee - 181*

## Why slow down?

There is a notion that doing multiple things at once to accomplish what we want will lead to a fulfilled life. Yet this is not the case. By slowing down, our lives will not become ineffective or dull and boring. We will have time to pause, to think, to enjoy and reflect. To weigh up decisions and to enjoy our relationship with others. We will be more capable of managing worry and anxiety by awakening in the present moment.

By slowing down, it becomes apparent that even if the world is chaotic; we just need to discover our own peace. More importantly, when we break our fast-paced habits, our relationship with God becomes healthy too. Our time spent with God becomes more like an intimate conversation that is not a routine or ritual. Guru Jee's words help us in having that conversation with God.

> You know the condition of my mind completely; who else could I go to tell of it? Without the Naam, the Name of the Lord, the whole world has become senseless; obtaining the Naam, it finds peace.
>
> *Guru Arjan Dev Jee - Sri Guru Granth Sahib Jee - 382*

Some of the methods that the Guru gives us to slow down are:

1) Start your day for God – we should work to live; we do not live to work, so we should not wake up just for work. Having a routine that is not just for weekdays but stays consistent at the weekend too really helps. Waking up before sunrise makes you efficient, and it enables you to connect at the time when your mind can quickly settle.

2) Show your love – when you meet someone, look for their good points and ignore their demerits. Focussing on the good, brings positive energy with it, which will help you accelerate much more quickly because love drives out negativity and is at the heart of finding God. Creating loving environments in

your life will also serve you back whenever you need support on this sometimes challenging path.

3) Accept God's Will – having control over your state of mind is tremendously powerful, especially when you are feeling that things are not going your way. Learn to ride the waves rather than drown in them. The ability to live in God's Will (called Hukam) builds resilience, acceptance and leads to contentment.

> Do not feel so delighted at the sight of wealth, and do not weep at the sight of suffering and adversity. As is wealth, so is adversity; whatever the Lord proposes, comes to pass.
> *Bhagat Kabeer Jee - Sri Guru Granth Sahib Jee - 337*

4) Sing the Guru's Words – one of the most beautiful things to keep you connected is the singing of the Guru's Words, this is called Shabad Keertan. There are Shabads (poetic verses) for every mood and every spiritual state that the mind is experiencing. You can select those that are in line with your stage in life, your spiritual level and your most prominent feelings.

5) Give with your hands – do something for others and make your life selfless rather than selfish. Earning an honest living will give you a feeling of happiness and achievement.

6) Watch, listen to and talk positively – engage in things that will help you rather than hinder you. Either remove or reduce the time you spend on those things that are keeping you from inner happiness. Box up negative thoughts to not spend time on them or reframe them to see the positive in situations. When things go wrong, don't just blame yourself for it. Try to find positives or become a better person from all the good and bad that happens. The Guru tells us that what we do with our thoughts, our words and our actions are what drive us. Make

all three of these work in your favour.

7) Build a supportive family unit - even if it is difficult to make significant changes, look for small changes that will all add up. For example, sit together as a family to eat and try to talk openly. Don't forget that change starts with yourself. Set an example and be a role model of support.

8) Monitor Your mental and physical health – to build your spiritual wealth, you need a healthy mind and body. Destress yourself regularly by learning about and doing activities that make you feel calm and relaxed. This awareness and approach will be your coping strategy for dealing with the ups and downs of life.

9) Talk to people – the best thing you can do to destress is speak to someone. You just need a listening ear. You do not require people to judge you in any way. You are unique, and your circumstances are too. Sometimes answers to problems come from inside when you speak openly about what is worrying you. Talk to your mind also; Gurbani does it all the time. You will be surprised at how your mind can solve its own problems when you let it settle.

# Questions to think over

What aspects of my life are going too fast and need slowing down?

What do I feel brings my mood down in life, and what can I do to overcome these things?

Is technology taking up too much of my time?

Which activities do I enjoy most and help me relax?

Of the nine tips that will assist me in slowing down, which ones am I doing or do I plan to do?

## What's next?

Slowing down is very important, so please take time to reflect and make healthy changes to your lifestyle. Next, you will get a chance to take an in-depth look into how your ego controls you and why you need to conquer it. Remember, Guru Jee talks about ego just as much as worship and Naam in Gurbani. You are at a significant part of your learning now because you will get an understanding of how your ego underpins everything. It has been controlling your drivers, your identity and directing your soul's journey. It is time you took back control!

# CHAPTER 6

# We have a toxic disease

### God or ego, never both

Our ego makes us self-centred, and it is the root cause of our separation from God. Guru Jee says it is a disease that lingers forever. Without a cure, our ego leads us through a never-ending cycle of transmigration.

> Engrossed in egotism, the world perishes. It dies and is re-born; it continues coming and going in reincarnation.
> *Guru Amar Daas Jee - Sri Guru Granth Sahib Jee – 33*

Ego drives us in virtually all aspects of life. Our frame of reference and viewpoint influences what we do. So we process information based on our identities, experiences, desires, attachments and biases. In most cases, all of these are selfish, so if we perceive and interpret the world like this, we push God aside to distinguish ourselves. We cannot be with God and be operating from our ego at the same time.

> When I am in my ego, then You are not with me. Now that You are with me, there is no egotism within me.

# The ego pollutes everything

Our ego drives everything that we do in life. We have been born because of it, and without Guru Jee's help, we will leave with it too. The ego's baggage accumulates and will remain with us, even when we die, causing us to be born over and over again.

> In ego, they come, and in ego, they go. In ego, they are born, and in ego, they die.
> *Guru Nanak Dev Jee - Sri Guru Granth Sahib Jee - 466*

We ask for happiness to fulfil our self-centred needs, but all worldly happiness attracts pain too. We also give and take with some selfish interest. For instance, we may do a task or give to someone because we require them in the future. When we commit sins, we know that our ego is driving us, but Guru Jee says we would never think that our truthfulness could be questionable too. Our ego can make us angry and cruel, so even though we are telling the truth, in reality, we want to be hurtful.

We do things with an ulterior motive which keeps us locked into materialism. In turn, our ego only respects those who have more than us or if they have a better reputation. We tend to look down upon those who have less than us. It gets worse because our ego makes us laugh in happiness and cry in sadness too. If we take laughing as an example, we may laugh at the expense of others. It is easy to find flaws in others, but it is easy to ignore our own. We usually find something funny if it happens to somebody else but would feel saddened if something similar were to happen to us.

## Removal of the ego

The good news is that the disease of our ego is curable. It starts by recognising how small and insignificant we are in God's command and creation.

> Everyone is subject to His Command; no one is beyond His Command. O Nanak, one who understands His Command, does not speak in ego.
> *Guru Nanak Dev Jee - Sri Guru Granth Sahib Jee - 1*

Our life and our circumstances are forever changing. The past is continually determining our present, and what we have today may not be there tomorrow. That is a good reason to treat others fairly and to not hurt them with our words or actions.

> Kabeer, do not be so proud and do not laugh at or mock the poor. Your boat is still out at sea; who knows what will happen?
> *Bhagat Kabeer Jee - Sri Guru Granth Sahib Jee - 1366*

As the ego stops driving what we say and how we think, our "I" gets eradicated. By removing our selfishness, the self-centred "I" dies and becomes "You", then we realise that God is in all things.

> Kabeer, repeating, "You, You", I have become like You. Nothing of me remains in myself. When the difference between myself and others is removed, then wherever I look, I see only You.
> *Bhagat Kabeer Jee- Sri Guru Granth Sahib Jee - 1375*

Everything we do should be in acceptance of God's Will. We do not laugh at the expense of others; instead, we feel a sense of happiness in watching God's play through creation. Our crying in no longer in self-pity, but in tears of separation instead.

> Whatever a servant of God does, they do it with love in the Will of God. Forever and ever, they abide with the Lord.
> *Guru Arjan Dev Jee- Sri Guru Granth Sahib Jee - 282*

Ultimately it is God's blessing that removes our ego. Whenever we do something right, the disease of ego seems to find its place in it by making us feel proud or better than others. Living life for God's blessing rather than for personal gain helps us cure the disease of ego.

> Such is the blessing that my beloved God has bestowed upon me. He has totally banished the five evils and the illness of egotism from my body.
> *Guru Arjan Dev Jee- Sri Guru Granth Sahib Jee - 716*

# Questions to think over

How has my ego polluted things in my life?

What role does my ego play when I give to others or expect from others?

Do I laugh or feel sadness because of my ego?

What am I doing to tackle ego in my life?

## What's next?

You are learning so much on your journey, congratulations! Subduing the ego is a huge task. Please take your time to learn and ask Guru Jee for help! So far, we have focused on the problem. The human body, our identity, our drivers, our actions, slowing down, the ego and much more! Now you will get a chance to understand what you can do to change your life—starting with why and how the Guru can help you. Only the Guru can remove our ego through a blessing called Gurprasad. You will learn that the Guru is more than just a teacher in your journey. The Words of Gurbani are magical, mystical and mesmerising! Learn why implementing them daily in your life is so central to liberating your soul.

# CHAPTER 7

# The guidance of the Guru

## Why do I need a Guru?

We learn from teachers in many aspects of our life. We go to school to learn our education, and at work, we get training or mentoring from professional bodies. We seek a qualified person who has relevant expertise in the field that we need help in. It is even more critical for us to be guided and taught in our spiritual life. In the Sikh faith, the Guru is more than just a teacher or a guide. Gurbani is also more than just words too.

> My True Guru, forever and ever, does not come and go. He is the Imperishable Creator Lord; He is permeating and pervading among all.
> *Guru Raam Daas Jee - Sri Guru Granth Sahib Jee - 758*

The light of the Guru is the light of God, and like God, the Guru does not die. God causes the Guru to speak the Words so that humans can be liberated.

O GurSikhs, chant the Naam, the Name of the Lord, night and day; through the True Guru, the Creator Lord will come to dwell within the home of your inner being. O GurSikhs, know that the Bani, the Word of the True Guru, is true, absolutely true. The Creator Lord Himself causes the Guru to chant it.

*Guru Raam Daas Jee - Sri Guru Granth Sahib Jee - 308*

Just like a qualified teacher, the Guru is qualified to teach us about liberation. The Guru is liberated from all entanglements and can guide us through our journey too.

I am a sacrifice, a sacrifice to such a Guru; He Himself is liberated, and He carries me across as well.

*Guru Arjan Dev Jee - Sri Guru Granth Sahib Jee - 1301*

Ordinarily, when we think about having a Guru, we automatically assume that it equates to losing control of our lives and the decisions made in it. In reality, although we may feel free, we are restricted and subject to our own conditioned beliefs. Our ego silently operates within its own narrow and selfish boundaries. So we are following a set of rules without being aware. The role of the Guru is to break down this wall of ignorance and guide us to the truth. Although obedience and discipline are required, the road is to liberation and not imprisonment!

Says Nanak, when the Guru tore down the wall of egotism, then, I found my Merciful Lord and Master. O mother! All my fears have been dispelled

*Guru Arjan Dev Jee - Sri Guru Granth Sahib Jee - 624*

## What does Guru Jee give you?

We say that the Guru liberates us, but what does that mean? First of all, the Guru nurtures our spiritual development. As with any good teacher, the Guru is compassionate and does not look at our faults. We are freed of our sins, negative thoughts and attachment to the world. We receive Naam from the Guru to unite us with God. And we receive protection from the Guru, who looks after our affairs in this world and the next. By removing our arrogance, Guru Jee leads us bliss and inner peace. We form a relationship with our soul, which we have neglected for so long.

> I am a sacrifice to my True Guru. I have come to understand my soul, and I enjoy supreme bliss. I have applied the dust of the Guru's Feet to my face, which has removed all my arrogant intellect. The Word of the Guru's Shabad has become sweet to my mind, and I behold the Supreme Lord God. The Guru is the Giver of peace; the Guru is the Creator. O Nanak, the Guru is the Support of the breath of life and the soul.
>
> *Guru Arjan Dev Jee - Sri Guru Granth Sahib Jee - 187*

## Gurbani – the Guru's Words

The collective writings of the Guru are called "Gurbani" and consist of thousands of Shabads. This scripture is called Guru Granth Sahib Jee and is given the same respect as if it were a living Guru. These writings are mystical, profound and enlightening since all of the writers of Gurbani had met God. Many Shabads describe that meeting along with the bliss that the soul experiences.

> Beholding the Blessed Vision, my mind has blossomed forth. And now everywhere I look, God is revealed to me.

Servant Nanak's hopes have been fulfilled by the Lord.
*Guru Arjan Dev Jee - Sri Guru Granth Sahib Jee - 176*

By serving the Guru, our spirit and personality rise above the darkness of Maya. When we surrender our ego and sacrifice ourselves to the Shabad, only then is our service accepted. Those who serve in this way are very fortunate.

> It is very difficult to serve the True Guru. Surrender your head; give up your selfishness. Realising the Shabad, one meets with the Lord, and all one's service is accepted. By personally experiencing the Personality of the Guru, one's own personality is uplifted, and one's light merges into the Light. Those who have such pre-ordained destiny come to meet the True Guru.
> *Guru Amar Daas Jee - Sri Guru Granth Sahib Jee - 27*

Gurbani nurtures us like a mother and father because the Guru and Gurbani are one. These Words become the interface between God and our lost soul by providing peace, truth and wisdom. Just like a mentor guiding us, it destroys our ignorance and purifies our sins.

> The Word, the Bani is Guru, and Guru is the Bani. Within the Bani, the Ambrosial Nectar is contained. If His humble servant believes and acts according to the Words of the Guru's Bani, then the Guru emancipates him.
> *Guru Raam Daas Jee - Sri Guru Granth Sahib Jee – 982*

To awaken our souls, Guru Jee asks us searching questions of which there are thousands in Gurbani. At times, the questions are for the mind. Other questions are a conversation with God. Some examples of questions are below:

- Why, O mind, do you plot and plan, when the Dear Lord Himself provides for your care?

- How can you forget the One who gave you your soul and the breath of life?

- When the body mingles with dust, what happens to the soul?

- How can honour be attained in His Court, if the Lord does not dwell in mind?

- You fool! Why are you so proud of Maya?

- O mind, how can you be saved without love?

# Questions to think over

What can I do to make my relationship with the Guru the most important in my life?

Thinking about my life, how could the Guru have helped me through some of the difficult times and experiences?

What kinds of service can I start doing to get closer to the Guru?

## What's next?

The Guru is central to everything that you do to meet God. Try to spend more time building up your relationship with Gurbani. To help, we will now look at how to stay connected to God. You will realise that you remain absorbed in worldly things quite easily. By redirecting this energy, you can keep your consciousness focussed, and with the Guru's blessing, you can reach a state of bliss that is unlike anything else you will experience.

# CHAPTER 8

# Staying connected

## The Gurmantar – more than just a word

The Guru tells us to stay lovingly connected to God night and day. Attaching ourselves in this way is not an easy task because it requires a great deal of effort and focus. There is not just one single method to remain connected. Gurbani talks about singing, praising, seeing God close by, contemplating on the Guru's word, and also trying to see God operating in the world and others. But one method that the Guru emphasises is "Jap", or the repetition of God's Name. This Jap, when underpinned by devotion to the Guru's path and a virtuous lifestyle, becomes a fast track route to connecting and merging with God.

The repetition of a mantar (commonly called "mantra") is a method that is available in many spiritual traditions. It is often a short word that is repeated by the tongue or silently in mind to bring about a positive sensation or feeling. Repetition builds strength, resilience and calmness. Usually, a mantra that refers to God focuses on just one aspect of God. For instance, God's creative power, God's giving power, God's merciful nature etc. In some traditions, the mantra could also be the direct worship of a deity or another part of creation. In the Sikh traditions, the mantra is a gift from the Guru, and not just a word that brings about positivity. It is called the Guru's mantra or "Gurmantar", and a Sikh receives this when initiated in a ceremony called "Amrit Sanchaar". This Gurmantar is given by five, practising Sikhs and the actual Name of God is "Vaheguru". The word breaks down into two parts; "Vahe" which means "wonderous bliss" and "Guru" which means "teacher that takes us out of darkness to the light". The Gurmantar unites us with God because it destroys our ego. It is not focussed on any particular attribute since God is infinite and is indescribable.

> The Guru-Mantar is 'Vaheguru', whose recitation erases egotism. Losing egotism and merging into the qualities of the Supreme Lord, he himself becomes full of qualities.
> *Bhai Gurdaas – Vaar 13 Pauree 2*

The aim is to merge with One, through single-minded focus and love. By repeating or singing the Gurmantar with the tongue and listening attentively with the ears, we remain absorbed internally.

> Hear with your ears, and sing with your tongue, and meditate within your heart on Him.
> *Guru Arjan Dev Jee - Sri Guru Granth Sahib Jee – 611*

As we build strength and our love increases, we can do this for longer and in different situations. The practice is simple, convenient and liberating because we can absorb ourselves in it regardless of where we are or what we are doing.

> While walking and sitting, sleeping and waking, contemplate within your heart, the Gur Mantar.
> *Guru Arjan Dev Jee - Sri Guru Granth Sahib Jee – 1006*

Repeating the Gurmantar becomes a very positive part of life. The essence of the Gurmantar is the same as that of Gurbani. They both contain the Amrit nectar, so when combined, they ignite our soul. This illuminated state will stay with us forever. The Guru tells us that those who serve God in this way remain connected, even at the time of death.

> During their life, they serve their Lord and Master, and as they depart, they keep Him enshrined in their consciousness.
>
> *Guru Arjan Dev Jee - Sri Guru Granth Sahib Jee – 1000*

When we are single-mindedly absorbed in God, that is called Naam. Naam is the energy that controls all of creation and looks over us during life's trials and tribulations, and when this life is over. When our inner-energy is low, it replenishes us, and when we are unsettled, it calms us. If we are feeling under pressure to solve an issue in our lives or at work, it will help us discover the most creative of solutions. When situations are bringing out the worst in us, the Gurmantar reminds us to handle the situation using Godly virtues rather than blame, hate and vengeance. Even those who are hostile towards us are tamed because the power of God's Name controls all of creation.

> Meditate on that Name of the Lord, O my mind, whose Command rules over everything. Chant that Name of the Lord, O my mind, which will save you at the very last moment. Chant that Name of the Lord, O my mind, which shall drive out all hunger and desire from your mind. Very fortunate and blessed is that Guru oriented person who chants the Naam; it shall bring all slanderers and wicked enemies to fall at his feet. O Nanak, worship and adore the Naam, the Greatest Name of all, before which all come

and bow.
*Guru Arjan Dev Jee - Sri Guru Granth Sahib Jee – 89*

There are many benefits to repeating the Gurmantar, but there is more to the Gurmantar practice than just mere repetition. While repeating God's Name, we must feel God's presence too. We start by recognising that we do not know how to do this, so we ask for God's blessing.

I do not know how to worship the Lord in adoration. I only repeat, "Har, Har, Guru, Guru."
*Guru Arjan Dev Jee - Sri Guru Granth Sahib Jee – 612*

By doing the following things when repeating God's Name, we can strengthen our practice and make our connection stronger.

See God as:

- the creator of all universes
- the giver to all of creation
- present in all of creation
- the cherisher and carer of all
- compassionate and merciful to the meek
- the ocean of peace who fulfils all hearts.
- all aware - He sees and hears everything and is always with me
- limitless and indescribable

Show your humility by:

- feeling that you have not appreciated God's virtues
- recognising your foolishness in thinking that God is far away
- feeling that God has saved countless sinners and will save you too

Guru Jee's instruction and the Gurmantar are a spiritual framework and attitude; therefore, the Guru warns us that just repeating a mantra without cultivating a sincere and honest heart will not bear fruit. Our attitude towards others and our sincerity to the Guru's instruction plays an essential role in our spiritual progress.

> One who chants the Har, Har, while continually practising deception, shall never become pure of heart. He may perform all sorts of rituals, night and day, but he shall not find peace, even in dreams.
> *Guru Raam Daas Jee - Sri Guru Granth Sahib Jee – 732*

## Doing two things at once

Our mind and body are not always pulling in the same direction. There are many times in life where we are physically doing some work or activity, yet, our inner focus is on something else. Drifting off in a short daydream is a perfect example of this, but often we centre on something more emotional, like a worry, a fearful thought or something exciting we are looking forward to doing. We can control the intensity of our inner focus and our outer focus in different proportions. Even when we are talking and interacting with others, our mind can remain attached to God.

> My mind is attached to the True Name. My dealings with other people are only superficial.
> *Guru Arjan Dev Jee - Sri Guru Granth Sahib Jee – 384*

One of the Shabads in Gurbani by a Saint called Naamdev describes how we can remember God while performing our day to day duties. Five real-world examples illustrate how different emotions make our mind focus on something while our outer body is doing something else.

- **The boy with the kite**

  The first example is of a boy who flies a kite while talking and laughing with his friends. His focus remains in the string even though he can continue enjoying the company of his friends. When the wind blows, he releases the kite string, and when it slows, winds the line in. He does this instinctively without much effort. Similarly, we can go about our daily duties while keeping our mind focused on our love for God.

- **The jeweller**

  A jeweller does some intricate work when making pieces of jewellery, yet deals with customers and purchases at the same time. The jeweller knows where he left off and what he has to do to complete the item. His mind remains attached to his work. Our connection with God is an occupation too, and Naam is the jewellery that we dedicate to creating beautifully.

- **The women carrying water pots**

  In India, fetching water is still prevalent where the provision of fresh running water is not available in the home. Women balance heavy pots of water on their heads while walking home. They do this very skilfully while continuing their conversations with their friends. With practice, they do not think about the pot – the balancing occurs naturally. Similarly, as we walk, talk and engage with others, we can still feel that inner energy and warmth for God.

- **The cow and her calf**

  Cows are very gentle animals that have a peaceful and sweet disposition. They have an intense connection with their calves and are very protective of their offspring. Grazing many fields away from her new-born, a cow remains distraught and unsettled until she gets reunited with it. Our feeling of separation from God can become intense too if we enshrine remembrance within our hearts and minds.

- **The mother and her baby**

  When a mother gives birth, she has an unbreakable maternal bond with her child. Even when working, talking, and sleeping, her mind stays connected with the baby. It is almost like she has developed a sixth sense for the baby. She goes about her daily chores, but her mind is always ready to attend to the needs of her child. This focused devotion is what we should strive for too.

Our memory and our emotions are both connected. In the previous examples, the boy does not want to lose his kite. The jeweller does not want to lose money by making an inferior piece of jewellery. The woman does not want to break the pot, and the mother does not want to see her baby suffer in any way and the cow worries for its offspring. Fear and love engage our mind to remember and focus.

> What would it matter, if my body were cut into pieces? If I were to lose Your Love, Lord, then Your humble servant would be afraid.
>
> *Bhagat Ravidaas Jee - Sri Guru Granth Sahib Jee – 486*

Practising this kind of remembrance is using a particular part of our minds called the "Chith". This part of our mind is primarily responsible for storing our memories and engaging our feelings. When we meet spiritual people, their "chith" remains connected, but they appear to be doing worldly things. Working hard as a householder and giving to others while staying connected is the way to meeting God. However, this way of living is not associated with a Godly life in many traditions. In India, even to this day, many traditions regard renunciation as the path to spirituality and liberation. A saintly person does not need to do this. They can be a householder, do work, raise children and experience Maya, without becoming attached to it.

> Remembering the True Lord in meditation, one is enlightened. Then, amid Maya, he remains detached. Such is the Glory of the True Guru; in the midst of children and spouses, they attain emancipation.
> *Guru Nanak Dev Jee - Sri Guru Granth Sahib Jee – 661*

Naamdev always seemed to be absorbed in his work and his saintly friend, Trilochan once asked him why. Naamdev gave the most beautiful response to Trilochan as he described how to do work and remain with God at the same time.

> Trilochan says, O Namdev, Maya has enticed you, my friend. Why are you printing designs on these sheets, and not focusing your consciousness on the Lord? Namdev answers, O Trilochan, chant the Lord's Name with your mouth. With your hands and feet, do all your work, but let your consciousness remain with the Immaculate Lord.
> *Namdev Jee - Sri Guru Granth Sahib Jee – 1375*

Initially, we have to dedicate a specific time, and we have to do this consciously. But ultimately, this way of remembrance does not require us to sit in isolation or assign a particular time. It becomes a way of life rather than a practice because it is our true nature to be connected to God.

## Remembering in times of difficulty

Remembering God in this way has further benefits and takes us out of distress when we face problems in life. The Guru outlines four types of pain that we face in life and reminds us that contemplation on God will comfort us and help us to handle these situations.

We sometimes have to face terrible hardships, and no one seems to offer any support. It feels as though friends turn into enemies, and even our relatives may desert us. If all support has given way, and all hope is lost, by remembering God with love, we will not be affected by any tribulation.

If financial hardships and money is causing us pain, and it feels as though we cannot achieve our hopes. If we are feeling unsuccessful, and none of our work gets accomplished, by remembering God, we receive the strength to overcome any obstacles in life.

In life, mental strain, stress, and anxiety can overtake us and even make our body feel unwell. The attachments of family life can become unbearable. Some days are joyful, while others are full of sorrow. Our sleep can become restless, and we feel lost. If we come to remember the Supreme Lord God, then our body and mind shall be cooled and soothed.

When lust, anger, greed and worldly attachment overpower us because of our selfish, egotistic mind. By being remorseful of our past, we can move our lives forward positively. If we do even a small amount of contemplation on God, we will be redeemed.

## Questions to think over

What am I spending the most time thinking about, and what emotion is associated with those thoughts?

What aspects of my day to day life distract me from being present and focussed?

What can I do to remember God when I am happy or when I have a problem in life?

Try and do an activity that you normally do but try staying focussing on God internally. How does it make you feel?

## What's next?

Naam is a beautiful gift that only the very blessed receive. Be thankful that you have had the opportunity to reflect on implementing it in your life. The more you love, the more you will receive. Next, you will get a chance to explore virtues and how to develop them. A virtuous life is a prerequisite for meeting God. We all have our own personalities, but you can always be a better person. A loving, sincere nature that is full of virtues is what will accelerate your journey.

# CHAPTER 9

# Cultivating virtues

## Theory vs practice

There seems to be a lot of admiration for living a spiritual life. Sometimes people get attracted to spirituality like it is a fashionable trend. The truth is that living a virtuous life is not about wearing a spiritual outfit for others to admire. We cannot just talk the talk. We must walk the walk too. It is easy to get absorbed in theories and methods, but how we practice and implement virtues in our daily lives is what truly matters.

> Truth is higher than everything, but higher still is a truthful life.
>
> *Guru Nanak Dev Jee - Sri Guru Granth Sahib Jee – 62*

Many examples are given to us by Guru Jee to help us understand this. If "sugar, sugar" were to be repeated there would be no sweet taste until we put sugar in our mouth. When we are ill, the doctor prescribes some medicine and the method in which to take it. If we do not take the medication as prescribed, our illness will remain and may even get worse. In the same way, the Guru reminds us to learn, understand but then live a virtuous life.

> Spiritual wisdom and contemplation all come from the Guru. Through the lifestyle of Truth, the True Lord comes to dwell in the mind. The self-willed manmukh (self-centred person) talks about it but does not practice it.
> *Guru Nanak Dev Jee - Sri Guru Granth Sahib Jee – 831*

As we transform both physically and internally, we are releasing lifetimes of baggage. There are going to be times when we have gained knowledge, but have not entirely implemented everything into our lives. It is impossible to learn everything about God, so we will always be behind the curve. But the point of learning is to destroy the ego by recognising how little we know. This creates the room that we need for virtues to grow.

> One thing can be placed into another thing, if it's contents are put aside first.*Guru Nanak Dev Jee - Sri Guru Granth Sahib Jee – 474*

## Virtues and true religion

Gurbani cautions the religious people that their religious rituals are of little use without cultivating virtues and removing the ego. Instilling God in our hearts is more important than empty rituals, which move us away from the food of the soul to give us a false sense of Godly living.

> Says Kabeer, now I know that the Lord dwells within the hearts of His Saints; that servant performs the best service, whose heart is filled with the Lord.
> *Bhagat Kabeer Jee - Sri Guru Granth Sahib Jee – 337*

## Muslim

Muslims worship at the mosque, have a prayer mat for daily prayer, revere the Quran, get circumcised and fast during Ramadan. The Guru's sermon to the Muslim is to connect with inner qualities to make this worship fruitful. Without virtues, all other things are of little value.

> Let mercy be your mosque, faith your prayer-mat, and honest living your Quran. Make modesty your circumcision, and good conduct your fast. In this way, you shall be a true Muslim.
>
> *Guru Nanak Dev Jee - Sri Guru Granth Sahib Jee – 140*

## Hindu

Hindus are required to wear a sacred thread of three strands called a Janou. Three strands represent a life of purity. Although this act is noble, a Janou is for the physical body in this world. Only virtues stay with the soul after this life.

> Make compassion the cotton, contentment the thread, modesty the knot and truth the twist. This is the sacred thread of the soul; if you have it, then go ahead and put it on me. It does not break; it cannot be soiled by filth; it cannot be burnt, or lost. Blessed are those mortal beings, O Nanak, who wear such a thread around their necks.
>
> *Guru Nanak Dev Jee - Sri Guru Granth Sahib Jee - 471*

## Yogi

Yogis live a secluded life in nature and wander from place to place.

Wearing a pouch, they go door to door, begging for food and often carry a walking stick. As they are also fond of music, they also have a stringed instrument. Yogis also master the eighty-four different yogic postures of the ancient Yoga system. Guru Jee beautifully tells the Yogi to make his body the neck of the instrument he plays, love and fear of God the strings and make the virtuous soul, or Gurmukh, the player.

> Make truth and contentment your plate and pouch, Yogi; take the Ambrosial Naam as your food. Make meditation your walking stick, Yogi, and make higher consciousness the horn you blow. Make your stable mind the Yogic posture you sit in, Yogi, and then you shall be rid of your tormenting desires. Go begging in the village of the body, Yogi, and then, you shall obtain the Naam in your lap… Make the Fear of God, and the Love of God, the two gourds of your lute, Yogi, and make this body its neck. Become Gurmukh, and then vibrate the strings; in this way, your desires shall depart.*Guru Amar Daas Jee - Sri Guru Granth Sahib Jee - 908*

## Some key virtues

To make our bodies pure and beautiful, we need to stop our sins and allow virtues to arise from inside. Our souls are a part of God, but our sins block out our virtues, and we become mesmerised in the illusion that the world presents to us.

> Pure is that body, in which sin does not arise. In the Love of the Lord is pure glory.
>
> *Guru Arjan Dev Jee - Sri Guru Granth Sahib Jee - 198*

**Fear**

Fear is a fascinating emotion because it is usually an unpleasant feeling that is a sign of weakness. But fear is one of the most crucial emotions for our development. We fear losing anything that we genuinely care about or respect. If we can develop our fear so that it prevents us from doing something that will be detrimental to us, it will help us focus our lives. We find God through true love, but it may come as a surprise that a precondition to love is to have fear. It is through fear that the treasure of love arises.

> Under Guru's Instruction, the Fear of God is produced, O Siblings of Destiny; true and excellent are the deeds done in the Fear of God. Then, one is blessed with the treasure of the Lord's Love, O Siblings of Destiny, and the Support of the True Name.
>
> *Guru Amar Daas Jee - Sri Guru Granth Sahib Jee – 638*

By remembering the fearless God, our fear disappears too. Fear gives rise to other virtues also, such as detachment, longing and even courage.

> When God instils His fear, a balanced detachment arises in the mind. Through this detachment, the Lord is obtained, and one remains absorbed in the Lord. *Guru Amar Daas Jee - Sri Guru Granth Sahib Jee - 490*

At the same time, fear also has to be controlled. It can be a weakness but also something that drives us in the wrong direction. Courageous people experience fear too. They just do not let it control their decisions. The nature of the mind is to fear, but we should not fear anything other than God.

Be afraid, if you have any fear, other than the Fear of God. Afraid of fear, and living in fear, the mind is held in commotion. *Guru Amar Daas Jee - Sri Guru Granth Sahib Jee - 490*

## Love

Love is a difficult emotion to describe. Our love for God is a blessing which comes when we lose our ego in the devoted congregation called "Sadh Sangat".

Without the Saadh Sangat, the Company of the Holy, love for the Lord does not well up; without this love, Your devotional worship cannot be performed. *Bhagat Ravidaas Jee - Sri Guru Granth Sahib Jee - 694*

Since it is quite challenging to describe love, the Guru has used practical examples to help us understand it.

- **The lotus flower** – is known as the most sublime of flowers because it sits in dirty water, yet it remains unpolluted and pure. When waves come, it remains steady. So the first attribute of love is to continue being attached even if by doing so, you receive discomfort or you feel pain.

- **The fish** – remains in the water and is happy, yet it dies very quickly if it removed from that water. The second element of love is to remain dependent on your Beloved, just like the fish is to water. It is then that you realise that you will die without that love.

- **The rainbird** – sings for a drop of water and does not stop until it gets one. Water may be everywhere surrounding it, but it only wants one drop of rain from the sky. This commitment to the One God is the third attribute of love

- **Water and milk** – when we heat milk to boil, the water

sacrifices itself first to save the cream. Love is a sacrifice of one's own needs for the preservation of another. When we love, we must give up something, whether it is time, effort, money or our personal preferences. Without sacrifice, there is no love.

- **The bird's sunrise** – in India there is a bird called a "Chukvi" that is fascinated by the sun. At night, the bird is separated from her beloved and continues to call. When the sun rises, she reunites with him, and her pain gets dispelled. In the same way, to love God, we must recognise our separation from Him. To continue to call Him through remembrance until we are reunited is a real sign of love.

## Forgiveness

When we hold on to hurt, we become emotionally unstable, and this can affect us and those around us in many ways. Our memories can become heavy baggage which always keeps our anger, negativity and unresolved emotions at the forefront of our lives. It also becomes very easy to slander those who have hurt you, which does not help us progress.

Forgiveness helps heal deep wounds from the past and is the perfect antidote for anger. Some research has shown that it can help reduce stress, depression, anxiety too. But, forgiving others is more than just a good quality with psychological benefits. It can bring God very close to us because truly forgiving someone is a Godly virtue.

> Where there is greed, there is death. Where there is forgiveness, there is God Himself.
>
> *Bhagat Kabeer Jee - Sri Guru Granth Sahib Jee – 1372*

**Humility**

Humility is the biggest weapon that we have against ego. True humility can only happen in the absence of the ego. It destroys arrogance and makes us more spiritually sensitive. Humility helps us remove conflict and understand those around us. Our personality should be like water which adapts to, enhances and helps the things that come in contact with it.

> As water flows downwards and also takes whatever mixes with it. Water adopts the colour of the dye that gets stirred with it. The actions of water are selfless and erase its ego. Wood does not drown in it. Instead, wood can even carry iron across. It brings prosperity in the rainy season by helping to ripen all types of fruit and vegetables. Likewise, the Holy Saints remain dead while alive. Removing their ego, their coming to the world is fruitful.
> *Bhai Gurdas Jee – Vaar 9 Pauree 20*

In humility we put the needs of others ahead of our own. By doing so, we experience virtues because they stem from humility. These virtues include empathy, gratefulness, kindness, sweet speech, charity and self-reflection.

When we start to see positive changes in our personality and lives, we need to remain cautious. We can learn a great deal from a true story about a Sanyasi (an Indian recluse) who during a lecture to an audience, spoke of his journey. He consistently talked about how he had "kicked people out of his life" to achieve his goals. He may have said this in different ways several times when someone in the crowd interrupted him. The man shouted, "You may believe that you have removed those people from your life, but in reality, they are still clinging to your leg!". It is easy to become proud of spiritual achievements because our pride does not allow us to let go of our weaknesses entirely; our arrogance still holds onto them. To experience humility, we must let go entirely and recognise that it is God's blessing, not our effort.

> Kabeer, what good is it to give up Maya, if the mortal does not give up his pride? Even the silent sages and seers are all destroyed by pride; pride consumes everyone.
> *Bhagat Kabeer Jee - Sri Guru Granth Sahib Jee – 1372*

# Questions to think over

Which virtues do I experience regularly and in what settings?

What do I fear the most? How can I make fear positive in my life?

Is love present in my relationships and my actions?

Have I forgiven those who have hurt me, or am I holding onto hurt?

What situations have occurred in my life where I could have been more humble?

## What's next?

As you live a virtuous life, you will feel happy and fulfilled. Your energy will also positively affect those around you. Saintly people are forever praised and revered in Gurbani! As you get closer to Vaheguru, you will enter a mystical world that takes you on a journey of bliss that you will not have experienced before. Read on to discover sounds, sights and tastes that will liberate you while you are alive!

# CHAPTER 10

# Transformation and mysticism

## Spiritual transformation

The goal of our life is to transform this human experience into a Godly one. We have to remove the layers of self-identity, hopes, desires, attachments and concerns to reveal our true self. All of this is possible through sacrifice to the Guru.

> A hundred times a day, I am a sacrifice to my Guru; He made angelic-beings out of men, without delay
> *Guru Nanak Dev Jee - Sri Guru Granth Sahib Jee – 462*

We give importance to how we are viewed in this world, yet we rarely think about how we will be considered in the next world. There may be a significant gap between how we conduct ourselves and what Guru Jee expects from us. When we give our love to Guru Jee, our shortcomings are ignored and removed, and we are placed on the right path. Through the Guru's Shabad, we become purified. We are then viewed very differently in the next world, and no longer have to return into rebirth.

> O True Guru, by Your Words, even the worthless have been saved. Even the most argumentative, vicious and indecent people, have been purified in Your company. Those who wandered in reincarnation and those who have been consigned to hell - even their families have been redeemed. Those whom no one knew, and those whom no one respected - they have become famous and respected at the Court of the Lord.
>
> *Guru Arjan Dev Jee - Sri Guru Granth Sahib Jee – 406*

## Enlightenment and intuition

The journey to meet God is a mystical and fascinating journey that is difficult to describe in words. Guru Jee emphasises that we must see God with our 'inner eye'. When we see God inwardly, we gain an understanding of how God operates in the outside world.

> He dwells inside, and outside as well. O Nanak, beholding the Blessed Vision of His Darshan, all are fascinated.
>
> *Guru Arjan Dev Jee - Sri Guru Granth Sahib Jee - 294*

To reach the inner state of enlightenment, we must open a hidden doorway which is in the body. Our body consists of nine visible doors. They are the eyes, ears, nostrils, mouth, and our organs for reproduction and releasing bodily waste. We have become accustomed to the tastes that we experience through the nine gates, but these flavours are bland and are not comparable to the experience of the tenth door.

> There are nine doors, but the taste of these nine doors is bland and insipid. The Essence of Ambrosial Nectar

trickles down through the Tenth Door.

*Guru Raam Daas Jee - Sri Guru Granth Sahib Jee - 1323*

We cannot see the tenth door physically; it must be discovered through self-control and focus. Guru Jee's teachings help us to realise it.

> The outgoing, wandering soul upon meeting the True Guru, opens the Tenth Gate. There, Ambrosial Nectar is food, and the celestial music resounds; the world is held spell-bound by the music of the Word. The many strains of the unstruck melody resound there, as one merges in Truth. Thus says Nanak: by meeting the True Guru, the wandering soul becomes steady and comes to dwell in the home of its own self.
>
> *Guru Arjan Dev Jee - Sri Guru Granth Sahib Jee - 577*

Our eyes, ears and tongue experience the physical world and enjoy the colours, attractions and entertainment. When an intense love and desire to meet God replaces these worldly attractions, then this new doorway is revealed.

> The Guru has shown me the hole, through which the deer-like mind carefully enters. I have now closed off the doors, and the unstruck celestial sound current resounds.
>
> *Guru Arjan Dev Jee - Sri Guru Granth Sahib Jee - 577*

Closing the doorways is not as simple as physically closing these outer doorways. When our focus is engrossed internally, we discover a new experience. This happens when the soul that experiences God is no longer satisfied with external involvements. The exterior doorways then close, but the inner doors are now truly open through the Guru's grace.

With my eyes, I have seen the world, but my great thirst is not quenched. O Nanak, those eyes are different, which behold my Husband Lord.

*Guru Arjan Dev Jee - Sri Guru Granth Sahib Jee - 577*

## Experiencing ecstasy

When the inner eyes see God, they are wonderstruck by the image of God, which is beautiful and perfect. By seeing God, we experience joy, peace, and bliss that is unlike any outer experience, even though it is impossible to put this experience into words.

He is so beautiful to my eyes; beholding Him, I have been wonderstruck.

*Guru Arjan Dev Jee - Sri Guru Granth Sahib Jee - 397*

Our ability to listen is one of our most important senses. The ability to listen is an ingrained part of life that allows us to connect to the world. The ears become engaged when they hear music and other enjoyable sounds. Gurbani tells us that when we get closer to God, we can listen to an unstruck melody or Anhad Shabad inside. This sound of this current is incomparable to anything that we can hear externally.

The unstruck sound current vibrates and resounds. The Lord's humble servants sing His Glorious Praises with love and delight; the Divine Guru honours them. The mind and body blossom forth in abundance when one receives even a drop of this Nectar. I cannot express His glory; I cannot describe His worth.

*Guru Arjan Dev Jee - Sri Guru Granth Sahib Jee - 892*

As our soul begins to merge with God, we experience the true meaning of Naam. The tongue stops craving sweet or stimulating flavours when it tastes the Amrit nectar; the sweetest taste of all.

> He alone comes to have it, whom the Guru blesses with this Ambrosial Nectar. The desire to eat, to wear new clothes, and all other desires, do not abide in the mind of one who comes to know the subtle essence of the One Lord.
> *Guru Arjan Dev Jee - Sri Guru Granth Sahib Jee - 892*

Our body is a beautiful machine consisting of atoms, cells, skin, nerves and many other tools for our survival. When we dig deep, there is a whole new world to discover that takes us to God. This journey is challenging, but Guru Jee tells us it is like nothing we will ever experience physically.

## Questions to think over

When I try to go beyond my outward experiences, what do I experience and how does it make me feel?

Does the time that I spend using technology affect my ability to go inwards?

What aspects of my life do I need to change to allow for my eyes, ears and tongue to experience the inner sights, sounds and tastes?

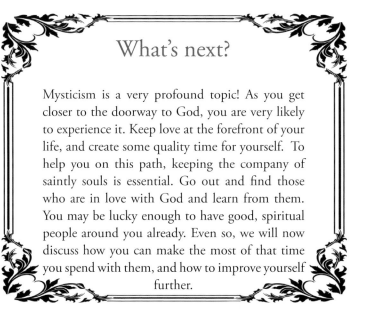

## What's next?

Mysticism is a very profound topic! As you get closer to the doorway to God, you are very likely to experience it. Keep love at the forefront of your life, and create some quality time for yourself. To help you on this path, keeping the company of saintly souls is essential. Go out and find those who are in love with God and learn from them. You may be lucky enough to have good, spiritual people around you already. Even so, we will now discuss how you can make the most of that time you spend with them, and how to improve yourself further.

# CHAPTER 11

# Saintly company

### How do my companions affect me?

The company that we keep will affect how we feel, think, act and speak. We have to interact with people in all walks of life, so if we surround ourselves with great company, it will benefit us in the long run. Those who we spend time with can make us better people and can help keep our spirits high. Unfortunately, they can also have an adverse effect on us too. Our behaviour is shaped by the traits of the company that we keep, so we must understand the importance of good company and the effects of bad company.

> Kabeer, do not associate with the faithless cynics; run far away from them. If you touch a vessel stained with soot, some of the residues will stick to you.
>
> *Bhagat Kabeer Jee - Sri Guru Granth Sahib Jee – 1371*

Saintly company is said to be like the fragrance of the sandalwood tree. Many cultures place great significance on the scent of the sandalwood tree. The aroma is so strong that it rubs off onto all the plants that surround it. Similarly, a person with good qualities positively affects those who sit in their company.

> Kabeer, the sandalwood tree is good, even though weeds surround it. Those who dwell near the sandalwood tree become just like the sandalwood tree.
>
> *Bhagat Kabeer Jee - Sri Guru Granth Sahib Jee – 1365*

## The company of Saintly people

In this dark age, it can be challenging to find good company. Singing God's praises in the company of saintly people is hugely important. Wherever two or more devotees of the Guru contemplate together, it is called the "Sadh Sangat", or the congregation of saintly people. The Sikh place of worship is a Gurdwara where the community gather. In a prayer called Sukhmani Sahib, Guru Jee talks about many benefits of going into such company and singing God's praises. Below are just a few of them.

1) **One's face becomes radiant** – when we leave this world, we still have a form. Our external body and physical features are temporary while we are on earth. Our spiritual face becomes radiant and glows when we reap the benefits of Sadh Sangat.

2) **All filth gets removed** – we are free of our sins and begin to recognise our true self. The dirt that we have accumulated through habits and vices is slowly washed away over time to reveal that true self.

3) **Egotism subsides**– the veil between God and us gets removed as we become one with the Sangat of saintly people. To determine if our ego is reducing, we must interact well with people. When we become humble in the Sangat, only then can we feel lower than everybody else in the world and

remove our ego.

4) **Spiritual wisdom gets revealed to us** – In the sanctuary of the Guru, we realise four important truths
   i) our real purpose in life
   ii) the workings of our mind
   iii) the actions that we need to do in our lives
   iv) how to interact with God and our soul

5) **God is understood to be near** – Guru Jee says that God is closer to us than our own physical hand. We begin to experience this through our inner feelings and life events. We also start to get answers to the difficult questions and challenges that confused us before.

6) **All conflicts cease** – in the holy congregation, there is no enemy and no friend. There is just the light of One. There is nothing to contest or divide, and there is no argument and no debate.

7) **One obtains the jewel of the Naam** – God is everywhere, and we start by discovering this through the singing of God's praises. Then by repeating God's Name. Duality gets removed, and the treasure of Naam gets revealed by the Guru. God is seen everywhere and in all events.

8) **One's efforts get redirected toward the One Lord** – we start to give our real goal the focus that it deserves. We think, speak and act in way prescribed by the Guru.

**Obtaining the fruits that the True Guru describes**

Guru Jee goes on to describe the Sadh Sangat as pure heaven where pain and suffering dispel and happiness is achieved. There are some specific things that we should do when we attend the Sadh Sangat.

- **Pray for a glimpse of God** – When we pray, sometimes we ask for worldly things, or sometimes we pray when we are thankful. There is nothing wrong with either of these things, but our primary goal in life is to meet God while alive. When we pray to meet God, we are asking for an experience called "Darshan". In the love of God, getting a glimpse of Him becomes the only desire.

Servant Nanak begs for this one gift: please bless me, Lord, with the Blessed Vision of Your Darshan; my mind is in love with You.
*Guru Arjan Dev Jee - Sri Guru Granth Sahib Jee - 959*

- **Create a routine** - Our daily routines usually revolve around work. We wake up for work rather than for God. A simple change is to wake up for Simran (contemplation on God) and prayer. Many Sikhs would go to the Sadh Sangat daily, having woken up early and done their Simran and prayers. Start waking up for God and keep your waking time consistent on the weekends too. It will change who you are and your life focus.

After taking your cleansing bath, remember your Beloved God in meditation, and your mind and body shall be free of disease. Millions of obstacles are removed, in the Sanctuary of God, and good fortune dawns.
*Guru Arjan Dev Jee - Sri Guru Granth Sahib Jee – 611*

- **Sacrifice yourself and show affection** –in Sadh Sangat, miraculous transformations take place because there is love for one other. To speak sweetly and to help others with true love is the path to happiness. If someone was to offer to pay off all of your financial debts, what would you give in return? You would probably feel indebted forever. Think about what we should sacrifice to that True Sangat who remove all of the adverse karma that has been accumulating for lifetimes and help us meet God! Guru Jee says we should offer our lives to them and serve them day and night!

If only someone would come, if only someone would come, and lead me to meet my Perfect True Guru. My mind and body, my mind and body - I cut my body into pieces, and I dedicate these to Him. Cutting my mind and body apart, cutting them into pieces, I offer these to the one, who recites to me the Words of the True Guru.
*Guru Raam Daas Jee - Sri Guru Granth Sahib Jee – 572*

- **See God in all** – It is difficult to comprehend that God is everywhere and in everybody. When we try and see the light of God in all, it has a humbling effect on our minds. A simple way of thinking about it is that the air we breathe is in everybody too! Just because we cannot see it does not mean it is not there. Guru Jee reminds us that in the Sadh Sangat, nobody appears to be wrong or bad. In this way, our evil-mindedness comes under control. Cherish the time and appreciate everybody – it will make your remembrance of God more satisfying and focussed.

You are constant in each and every heart, and in all things.
O Dear Lord, you are the One.
*Guru Raam Daas Jee - Sri Guru Granth Sahib Jee – 10*


- **Use the Words of Gurbani** - Guru Jee's words are the

"lighthouse" in this world because they dispel darkness. The Words are the complete guide to contemplation and spirituality. We can use Gurbani as a gauge to establish where we are on our journey, and how effectively we are utilising our time in the Sadh Sangat.

Gurbani is the Light to illuminate this world; by His Grace, it comes to abide within the mind.

*Guru Amar Daas Jee - Sri Guru Granth Sahib Jee – 67*

- **Keep the focus on One** – Everything emanates from One, and everything is connected by One. God is Oneness that permeates the entirety of creation and beyond. There is only One God that sustains all. To see this Oneness, we need to focus single-mindedly on God.

He Himself is the One and only; from the One, the One and only, came the expanse of the entire creation.

*Guru Arjan Dev Jee - Sri Guru Granth Sahib Jee – 379*

**Inspire others and reach out** – As you progress, share your happy experiences and welcome others to the Sadh Sangat. Socialising builds self-esteem in both you and others and gives everyone a sense of belonging. Happiness and contentment have a positive effect on the atmosphere and those in the Sadh Sangat.

Those, within whom the Truth dwells, obtain the True Name; they speak only the Truth. They walk on the Lord's Path and inspire others to walk on the Lord's Path as well.

*Guru Raam Daas Jee - Sri Guru Granth Sahib Jee – 140*

## Questions to think over

What company do I keep and how has it come into my life?

Do I feel some of the things that Guru Jee says we experience when I sit in a spiritual congregation?

How can I give more to the Saadh Sangat to make my spiritual progress?

## What's next?

Guru Jee says that even the religious books cannot describe the benefits of keeping saintly company. Sadh Sangat is a beautiful place to keep you connected, so please make the most of it.

We are born to be generous, kind and appreciative. You will now learn about how to serve effectively, being grateful for what you have, and being generous with what you can offer. We started off learning about our selfish attachments and desires. This section will teach you about the cure!

# CHAPTER 12

# Serving selflessly

## Serving is our purpose

Our natural inclination is to focus on what is lacking in our lives to try and fill the gap. We all do what we feel is essential for our needs, so we chase the things that will give us, and those we care for, comfort. Our drive is for more in life because that is what gets noticed, and that is what will make us better off. We encourage our children to achieve their university qualifications and get a high paying job. To continue the cycle of wealth and influence in hopes that they too, will be comfortable.

There's nothing wrong with working hard; in fact, it is encouraged by Guru Jee. Achieving financial success can also be very beneficial. And there is certainly nothing wrong with having influence. What matters is how we make use of all of these things while living this human life.

> Without service, cursed are the hands and feet, and useless are other deeds.
>
> *Bhai Gurdaas – Vaar 27 Pauree 10*

Without serving, we invite selfishness into our hearts. But when we delve into why people are charitable it becomes evident that a selfish motive can also drive serving. We sometimes lose all of the benefits of our service when our desire is not selfless and pure in heart.

> In the minds of the charitable, contentment is produced, thinking about their giving. They give and give, but ask a thousand-fold more in return, and hope that the world will honour them.
> *Guru Nanak Dev Jee - Sri Guru Granth Sahib Jee – 465*

Before we give to charitable causes, it is vital to ensure that we have earned our wealth honestly. Wealth obtained from lies, deception and exploitation does not get washed clean if we try to do good with it. In India, it has been common practice for centuries to give offerings in the name of ancestors who have passed away. Guru Jee explains that the actual fruit of offerings is in the purity of the earnings, rather than the amount given, regardless of how noble a cause it may be.

> The thief robs a house and offers the stolen goods to his ancestors. In the world hereafter, this is recognised, and his ancestors are considered thieves as well.
> *Guru Nanak Dev Jee - Sri Guru Granth Sahib Jee – 472*

Those who genuinely serve others do so because of gratitude and generosity. Both of these virtues strengthen our mental, spiritual and physical well-being. Earning an honest living, being thankful through the remembrance of God and giving selflessly to others without desire for a reward; these are the three core principles of a healthy, spiritual life.

# Gratefulness – a powerful catalyst for happiness

We should be thankful to the world, to people around us and most importantly, to God for all that we have. There are lots of things that we should be grateful for. We have a house, food, wealth, family, friends, a healthy body, cosy beds, clothes; the list goes on. Gratitude does not come easy to us because we have many forces that feed our selfishness. For instance, the drive to get more material wealth, believing it will make us happier. By being so fixated on what we do not have, we become ungrateful, resentful and selfish. A constant focus on these things will not allow us to appreciate the benefits of helping others. These are sure signs that we have forgotten Vaheguru, who is the actual provider.

> He obtains ten things, and puts them behind him; for the sake of one thing withheld, he forfeits his faith. But what if that one thing was not given, and the ten things were also taken away? Then, what could the fool say or do?
> *Guru Arjan Dev Jee - Sri Guru Granth Sahib Jee – 268*

By appreciating what we have, rather than focusing on what we do not have, we start to recognise blessings in our lives. If our environment and our attitude encourage us to remember God, then we are incredibly fortunate.

> That time, that moment, that instant, that second is so fruitful, O my soul, when my Lord comes into my mind.
> *Guru Raam Daas Jee - Sri Guru Granth Sahib Jee – 540*

Those who are grateful can see happiness in almost any situation. We don't take things for granted even when things are not going our way. Learning to ride the waves of daily life in this way allows us to see God's wonders happening around us.

> By His Grace, you listen to the sounds of the world and
> nature.
> By His Grace, you behold amazing wonders.
> By His Grace, you speak ambrosial words with your
> tongue.
> By His Grace, you abide in peace and ease.
> By His Grace, your hands move and work.
> By His Grace, you are entirely fulfilled.
> By His Grace, you obtain the supreme status.
> By His Grace, you are absorbed into celestial peace.
> Why forsake God, and attach yourself to another?
> By Guru's Grace, O Nanak, awaken your mind!
> *Guru Arjan Dev Jee - Sri Guru Granth Sahib Jee – 270*

## Being generous

Generous people are kind, sincere and selfless. Even if they do good, their mind does not dwell on it. They do not want to receive anything in return for their efforts, and often they will serve those who may have even hurt them in the past. A generous person is like a tree that suffers pain at the hands of people, but it continues to give them fruit.

> They endure suffering themselves but pour happiness on
> the world. Even on being stoned, a tree offers its fruits and
> removes hunger.
> *Guru Arjan Dev Jee - Sri Guru Granth Sahib Jee – 270*

When people are cruel and unfair towards us, it is easy to seek revenge and respond with. Saintly, generous souls do not react in this way. They can see that evil-doers need help as they are only ruining themselves. By not responding negatively, they remain physically and mentally healthy also.

> Fareed, respond to an evil-doer with goodness; do not fill your mind with anger. Your body shall not suffer from any disease, and you shall obtain everything. *Fareed Jee - Sri Guru Granth Sahib Jee – 1381*

Generous acts are not just rituals or routines. They come from an attitude of selflessness and genuine compassion. In this world, it sometimes feels that we receive a form of punishment for doing good. Acts of generosity will often be ignored, undermined and sometimes misinterpreted. This does not matter, because God sees, hears and responds to everything. The fruits of what we do on earth will also be received when we leave this world.

> In the midst of this world, do Seva – selfless service, and you shall be given a place of honour in the Court of the Lord.
> *Guru Nanak Dev Jee - Sri Guru Granth Sahib Jee – 25*

# Questions to think over

What am I grateful for in my life, and in what ways do I show this gratitude?

Are there things in my life that I should be more appreciative of?

How do I feel when I help others?

What am I doing, or can I do, to serve others selflessly?

## What's next?

Well done! You are getting close to reaching the end of this learning journey. Hopefully, you have learned a great deal, and are a better person for it. We have been talking about God throughout this book. Don't live your life treating God like a concept or an idea. Find ways of getting closer and experiencing God. You will now have an opportunity to get to know a bit more about what is pleasing to God.

# CHAPTER 13

# Knowing Vaheguru

We can spend many years believing in God without developing a personal relationship. When things do not go well in life, our relationship may weaken because we feel distant. Over time, our prayers can also become routine and lose their emotional impact. Those who have formed a strong relationship tell God everything about their life and their feelings. Gurbani helps us to understand God and build up this relationship through love and devotion.

> My conversation is with the One Lord alone; He never frowns or turns His face away. He alone knows the state of my soul; He never ignores my love.
> *Guru Arjan Dev Jee - Guru Granth Sahib Jee – 958*

**Make your prayer a conversation**

Gurbani enables us to talk to God through our prayers. Certain Shabads speak directly to God, some to the Guru, others are a conversation with the Sadh Sangat or the mind. When we read Gurbani, how we say the words will have a significant effect on our souls. By talking directly to God through our prayers, we can form a very close relationship with God in this way.

> You are my Companion; You are my Best Friend. You are my Beloved; I am in love with You. You are my honour; You are my decoration. Without You, I cannot survive, even for an instant.
>
> *Guru Arjan Dev Jee - Guru Granth Sahib Jee – 181*

## Understanding what is pleasing to God

In the world today, there is a vast array of rituals, music, songs, specific scriptures, and religious codes which on their own, will not bring us closer to God. We can spend our life using many methods without understanding what is pleasing to God. Wisdom, knowledge and meditation techniques are not sufficient. Many abandon the world, live in the wilderness or visit sacred shrines. Some give huge donations feeling that this is the way to please God. Guru Jee says God is pleased only through self-surrender. There are specific pointers in the Guru's message that guide us in the right direction.

### See God nearby
Whatever we do, and wherever we are, we should try to feel that God is forever present.

> O Nanak, that soul-bride is pleasing to her Husband Lord, who, through the Shabad, remains in His Presence.
>
> *Guru Amar Daas Jee - Guru Granth Sahib Jee – 567*

### Say God's Name with oneness in mind, body and speech.
Our mind, body and words should say God's name in oneness. There should be no desire or need other than to meet God.

One who speaks the Lord's Name, with mind, body and mouth, is pleasing to the Lord.

*Guru Amar Daas Jee - Guru Granth Sahib Jee – 567*

## Surrendering our ego to the Guru

To kill our ego, we cannot partially surrender it to the Guru. Falling at the Guru's feet means that we need to give up our wisdom completely.

The Supreme Lord God is pleased with those who fall at the Guru's Feet.

*Guru Amar Daas Jee - Guru Granth Sahib Jee – 592*

## Give up your pride and arrogance

Argumentative, stubborn and proud personalities are not pleasing to God. They undo any good that we do and keep us bound to our ego.

If a servant performs service while being vain and argumentative, he may talk as much as he wants, but he shall not be pleasing to his Master.

*Guru Angad Dev Jee - Guru Granth Sahib Jee – 474*

## Become the dust of the saintly

We give up our rigid personality when we feel like we are the dust of those who serve and live for God.

That service is pleasing to Him when it is done humbly by becoming the dust of the feet of the Saints.

*Guru Arjan Dev Jee - Guru Granth Sahib Jee – 136*

## See life and death as one journey

Life and death are just a chapter for our soul. These events do not define us. Our soul does not die, so a real connection with God gets created when we are not concerned with the journey of the body.

> One who looks alike upon death and birth is pleasing to my God.
> *Guru Amar Daas Jee - Guru Granth Sahib Jee – 1058*

<u>Fight and conquer your vices</u>
Our five weaknesses overtake and drive us away from God. So as we start to remove our association with them, God gets closer.

> Conquer sexual desire, anger, greed and worldly attachment; only such a game as this is dear to the Lord.
> *Guru Arjan Dev Jee - Guru Granth Sahib Jee – 1185*

## Understand your place in the world

As our love grows, we realise that God is not just "someone" who does not let bad things happen to us. We understand that we are in a difficulty that we have created for ourselves. Our feelings of sadness or happiness are just temporary. Vaheguru is always with us to helps us manage those challenges and come through to find true happiness.

> …Do not blame anyone else; blame your own actions instead. Whatever I did, for that I have suffered; I do not blame anyone else.
> *Guru Nanak Dev Jee - Guru Granth Sahib Jee – 432*

## Be a true friend

Our approach towards the world is one of tolerance and harmony. People form a unity for many different reasons. If we connect with the world through oneness, then the gaps that we have created between humanity get removed. God is in creation, so oneness with God cannot happen without oneness with the world too.

> I am a friend to all; I am everyone's friend. When the sense of separation was removed from my mind, then I was united with the Lord, my King.
>
> *Guru Arjan Dev Jee - Guru Granth Sahib Jee – 671*

## Remain content in God's Will

When we wait for joy to come to us, it never really does. To know God, we must accept everything that happens is in His Will. This does not mean that we sit back and do not strive to achieve in life. It just means that we do not have lots of filters that call things wrong. There is no need to compare what we have with others. By developing this mindset, happiness can start today without the need to change too much. If things are not looking great, then like the lotus rides the turbulent waves but remains steadfast, our steadiness in turmoil should be our trust in God.

> If You bless me with happiness, then I will worship and adore You. Even in pain, I will meditate on You. Even if You give me hunger, I will still feel satisfied; I am joyful, even amid sorrow.
>
> *Guru Raam Daas Jee - Guru Granth Sahib Jee – 757*

## Live a life without fear

We always fear the worst in life. We may be fearful of being hurt, dying, or of something terrible happening to those who we love. Fear is a natural emotion that alerts us of a threat or danger. Having faith in God makes our emotional response to fear unique. Nothing can happen in this world without God's command, so what should we be afraid of in life? We know that fear is part of creation and that God is fearless. Our body is subject to fear, but our soul is not, so through this understanding, we naturally become fearless too.

> Old age, death, fever, poisons, and deadly snakes - everything is in the Hands of the Lord. Nothing can touch anyone without the Lord's Order. Within your conscious mind, O servant Nanak, meditate forever on the Name of the Lord, who shall deliver you in the end.
>
> *Guru Raam Daas Jee - Guru Granth Sahib Jee – 168*

## Questions to think over

How have events in my life affected my relationship with God?

What efforts am I making to be pleasing to God?

By becoming a true friend, God becomes your friend. In what ways am I a friend to the world and to the people around me?

### What's next?

Congratulations! You have reached the end of this brief learning journey. You now have a better understanding of what true salvation is and how you can meet God in this life through the Guru's blessings. I hope that the truth and the wisdom that the Guru has imparted on you will have a lasting effect on your life. Remember, this is just the start of your learning! The ocean of Guru Granth Sahib Jee is waiting for you to explore it. I will leave you with some tips for your life journey that you can start to implement today. Good luck on your journey! Even though there is no such thing as luck!

# CHAPTER 14

# Ten things to change your life today

### 1.  Wake up early

Wake up during the early hours of "Amrit Vela,"; the last phase of the night. Doing so will be very beneficial for your spiritual growth. Day and night break down into eight parts that are each three hours in length. As you build up your focus by awaking in the final period of the night, three hours before sunrise, you will begin to connect more easily. At this time, your mind will settle more quickly, and your surroundings will be quiet too. After a good, healthy sleep, your body will have rested, and the rhythms generated at this early hour will help you connect. The practice of waking at Amrit Vela is a stepping stone to your bigger goal, which is to stay connected day and night.

> In the fourth watch of the early morning hours, a longing arises in their higher consciousness. Their friendship is with the river (for bathing), the True Name is in their minds and on their lips.

## 2. Protect your Amrit nectar

When you connect with your higher consciousness, you will gather Amrit nectar. Sing, read and chant praises with all of your love, then you will feel an inner change that is uplifting and comforting. When you allow yourself to go back into Maya, you will lose it again. Your ego will try to redirect you into worldly distractions, and the Amrit nectar will become distant. This is why you will then feel separated from God. Remain conscious of God in everything that you do to protect the precious nectar that you have collected.

> By removing the desire for another's wealth, physical beauty, and slander, I have now enshrined meditation on the Lord's name, charity, and inner and outer cleanliness. Through the teachings of the Guru, I have restrained my mind from going astray.
>
> *Bhai Gurdas Jee – Vaar 29 Pauree 2*

## 3. Give to the needy

Earn an honest living and then giving one-tenth of your earnings to selfless service. In this way, you will break away from your attachment to wealth. Be thankful for everything that you have, and be generous to others.

> One who works for what he eats, and gives some of what he has -O Nanak, he knows the Path.
>
> *Guru Nanak Dev Jee - Sri Guru Granth Sahib Jee – 1245*

## 4. Forgiveness is to be God-like

To get close to God, you need to learn to forgive. Remind yourself daily that you are the light of God. Then remember that the same light is also in others. Wish good on those who do wrong to you. See no enemy in anyone and be a good friend.

Kabeer, where there is spiritual wisdom, there is righteousness and Dharma. Where there is falsehood, there is sin. Where there is greed, there is death. Where there is forgiveness, there is God Himself.

*Bhagat Kabeer Jee - Sri Guru Granth Sahib Jee – 1372*

## 5.  Company of the saintly

Keep the company of those who are on the spiritual path too. Use different tools and opportunities to stay connected to them. Be aware of negativity and ensure that the company that you keep is keeping your mind healthy and positive. Remember that you can also use books and technology to connect with others.

The treasure of the Name is in the Sat Sangat, the True Congregation. There, the Lord is found. By Guru's Grace, the heart is illuminated, and darkness is dispelled.

*Guru Nanak Dev Jee - Sri Guru Granth Sahib Jee – 1244*

## 6.  See God in everything

How you perceive your surroundings is a reflection of your inner-self. What you see is based on your perception of who you are and what is important to you. When you feel closer to God inside, then God will feel near to you in all parts of your life. You are never alone, and you are not separate from the world – the unifying light of God is always with you.

Wherever I look, there I see Him present; He is never far away. He is all-pervading, everywhere; O my mind, meditate on Him forever. *Guru Arjan Dev Jee - Sri Guru Granth Sahib Jee – 677*

## 7.  Do not use hurtful speech

Hearts are like diamonds, so to hurt someone with harsh words is like breaking God's heart. If you use hurtful speech, your mind and body will be affected negatively. Slandering, backbiting, and using profanity are examples of speech which is detrimental to your spiritual progress. Your body is like a field in which you are planting the seeds of your actions. Any harmful speech will turn your body into a barren land where even the seeds of your better deeds will not bear fruit. Remember that you are part of God. It is your nature to be sweet and humble. Do not let others bring you down or distract you from this.

> Do not utter even a single harsh word; your True Lord abides in all. Do not break anyone's heart; these are all priceless jewels. The minds of all are like precious jewels; to harm them is not good at all. If you desire your Beloved, then do not break anyone's heart.
>
> *Farid Jee - Sri Guru Granth Sahib Jee – 1384*

## 8.  Help others

As a spiritual seeker always do good for others. Make it part of your life to help others on their spiritual path. Helping could be anything from giving them resources to kick-start their journey, socialising with them, meditating together, or just having positive, spiritual conversations.

> O, my Lord, I am a sacrifice to the humble servants of the Lord. I make my hair into a fan and wave it over them; I apply the dust of their feet to my face. Those generous, humble beings are above both birth and death. They give the gift of the soul and practice devotional worship; they inspire others to meet the Lord.
>
> *Guru Arjan Dev Jee - Sri Guru Granth Sahib Jee – 748*

### 9. Do less to gain more!

Be conscious of how much you eat, sleep, and talk. Overindulgence in these three things will bind you to the world. By reducing them to a level that you *really* need, you will open up the door to realisation. You will also create a foundation for your spiritual growth.

> Eat less and sleep little, cherish mercy and forgiveness.
> Have a gentle personality, stay content, and remain free
> from three modes of Maya.
>
> *Guru Gobind Singh Jee - Dasam Granth Sahib Jee – 709*

> They speak sweetly, act humbly and get happiness from
> serving with their hands for the well-being of others. Sleeping,
> eating and talking less, they adopt the teachings of the Guru.
>
> *Bhai Gurdas Jee – Vaar 28 Pauree 15*

### 10. Learn more to improve yourself

Read Gurbani, the Guru's Words, and learn from them. Keep a journal and try to measure your changes and improvements over time. These words are the ocean of knowledge that will steer your mind out of duality. Contemplate on everything that you have learned and try to implement the teachings into your daily life. In this way, humility, simplicity, kindness, and love will come into your life which will protect you in this world and the next.

> The Word of God's Bani, The Shabad, is the best
> utterance. So continually sing it, listen to it, and read it,
> O Siblings of Destiny, and the Perfect Guru shall save you.
>
> *Guru Arjan Dev Jee - Guru Granth Sahib Jee – 611*

# CHAPTER 15

# Interesting facts about the Sikh faith

In 1469, Guru Nanak came to the world at a time when social, religious, cultural and communal divisions were widespread. Guru Nanak travelled far and wide, spreading the message of divinity to save the world.

> Guru Nanak is the greatest of all; the Guru has saved my honour in this Dark Age called Kalyug.
> *Guru Arjan Dev Jee - Sri Guru Granth Sahib Jee - 749*

Often, spiritual writings and religious texts are written many years and sometimes centuries after those who uttered them. The uniqueness of Gurbani is that it is not an account of their lives that was written years after they left this world. Gurbani is the first-hand account of the divine message that was written by the Gurus and Saints while they were here on earth.

> The Bani of His Word emanated from the Lord. It eradicates all anxiety.

Sikhs are a highly visible community with a clear physical identity and code. For most Sikhs, a significant part of their journey starts with their outer appearance and outwardly practices, such as wearing a uniform and a turban while following a code of conduct and a daily routine. A summary of the interesting points about the traditions appears at the end of the book.

❊  Sikhs believe in One Immortal God, who is beyond description and names. God has been given names based on attributes, such as being the creator and the sustainer of the world, the forgiver of sins, and one who protects the weak.

❊  Ten Gurus between 1469 and 1704 founded the faith. Each Guru was regarded as the "Joth of Guru Nanak," indicating that the same Light was passing through each Guru. For Sikhs, this "Light" now resides in Guru Granth Sahib Jee, the revered scripture that is the final Guru for the Sikhs.

❊  Guru Granth Sahib Jee contains the writings of six of the ten Gurus. The Shabads of other mystical and saintly souls, whose experiences resonated and aligned with the Guru's message are also present in Guru Granth Sahib Jee.

❊  The Sikh Scriptures are fascinating in that the structure of the arrangement is in musical modes called Raags. One of the beauties of Guru Granth Sahib Jee is that writings of Saints other than the Gurus also have a parallel seat in the scriptures. Guru Granth Sahib Jee is a unique lighthouse of wisdom that transcends social structures, religion, and other dividing factors. The barriers that ironically still plague India and the world to this day.

❊  Sikhi is a unique faith where Guru Granth Sahib Jee was

written and finalised by the Gurus themselves. Of all other major religions in the world, their holy scriptures were not written or finalised by their founder. Rather, they were written by followers sometimes hundreds of years after their founder's death, leading to variations of the original message.

✻ The writings of Guru Granth Sahib Jee are called Gurmukhi, which means "spoken by the Guru."

✻ A Sikh place of worship is called a Gurdwara. The most popular Gurdwara is the Harmandhir Sahib, also known as the Golden Temple, where more than 100,000 devotees visit every day. This makes it the most visited place in the world.

✻ Sikh initiation happens through a ceremony known as "Amrit" or "Amrit Sanskaar." The tenth Guru, Guru Gobind Singh Jee, initiated 5 Sikhs in 1699 after asking them to give up their attachment to the world and to offer their heads as a sacrifice. They passed the test, so this courage became the foundation for initiation. Anyone can become a Sikh, and when initiated, are also called the Khalsa.

✻ Five Sikhs who lead a disciplined life carry out the ceremony. Those who present themselves for initiation receive Amrit if they are committed to living a saint-soldier life. Anyone can become a Sikh if they accept the tenets of the faith.

✻ Sikhs do not cut their hair as a sign of acceptance of God's will and also as an identity. The hair or Kesh, when uncut, also has spiritual and health benefits too.

✻ A turban is worn to keep hair covered. The turban is called a Dastar and consists of two parts. The smaller turban is worn under the main turban and is called a Keski. It is used to keep the head covered when sleeping, bathing and at other times when wearing a large turban is not practical.

✳ They also wear an iron bangle (Kara), a small ceremonial sword (Kirpan), a comb (Kanga), and special underwear (Kashera). This forms the Sikh's uniform as a saint-soldier, one who is prepared to sacrifice themselves to uphold truth and to protect others.

✳ They contemplate and repeat God's Name daily before sunrise, having had their daily bath. A Sikh prays three times a day by performing five prayers at dawn (Jap Jee Sahib, Jaap Sahib, Tvai Prasad Svaiye, Chaupai Sahib and Anand Sahib), one prayer in the evening (Rehraas Sahib), and one before sleeping (Sohila Sahib).

✳ Saying God's Name in remembrance is not just a form of mantra meditation. A Sikh will try to use each breath to enshrine love into the deepest part of their consciousness. By detaching from ego and applying love and fear, they try to remain God-conscious day and night. The purpose is to try and see God operating in nature, in creation, in daily events and the hearts of all. This Naam becomes their friend, family and companion.

✳ There are also four cardinal sins that a Sikh must not commit. The removal or cutting of hair on the body, eating of meat, committing adultery and consuming intoxicants such as drugs, tobacco and alcohol are forbidden.

✳ Emphasis on earning an honest living through hard work is essential. Therefore, gambling in the form of lottery, casinos, or similar activities is contrary to the teachings of the faith.

✳ To conquer the five evils of lust, anger, greed, attachment and ego. To ignite the Godly virtues of truth, contentment in oneness, compassion, righteous conduct, patience, and forgiveness are the core spiritual goals of life.

* A Sikh regards the whole of the human race as equal. No person is considered low due to their caste, creed or family lineage.

* To receive God's blessing and to recognise that God operates in all things, Sikhs start tasks and work with a prayer. The daily routine revolves around God-awareness. Sikhs also pray on waking, during the day, in the evening and before sleep. The goal of each of these routines is to realign focus to God-consciousness. Any new task or job commences with a prayer. What we eat also affects our spiritual state. Some dedicated Sikhs only eat food that has been made by practising Sikhs while focusing on the Guru's Shabad during preparation.

* The faith encourages a very healthy and honest lifestyle of natural food and a simple diet. Over-eating and eating unhealthy food is to be avoided. By not hurting anything or anyone and sharing with others, a Sikh aims to live in harmony with all.

* A Sikh has no desire for liberation after death. The aim is to liberate the soul while alive by combatting the five passions and attaining God qualities. Death is considered a blissful event and not something that should be feared.

* Sikhs refrain from idol worship and do not bow down to statues, pictures or graves. They have no faith in horoscopes, astrology, gemstones, good or bad days or other superstitions.

* There are four main ceremonies which are the baby naming ceremony, the initiation ceremony, the marriage ceremony and finally the funeral ceremony.

* To remain connected with God, to earn an honest living and then to share those earnings are the base principles for a Sikh.

To take responsibility for their family needs and the needs of society are integral to being a Sikh. One-tenth of earnings should go to selfless causes.

✱ Where other faiths believe that you meet God after dying, Sikhs believe that you can meet God whilst alive.

# GLOSSARY

Amrit Nectar the divine nectar that is revealed in the body
Amrit Sanskaar initiation ceremony in the Sikh traditions
Amrit Vela the last 3 hours before sunrise when devotees wake-up
Chith the part of the mind that remembers and has emotions
Chukvi a bird that is fascinated by the sunrise and remains awake
Darshan experiencing the vision of God
Dharma the path of righteouness and virtues
Divine Light the light of God which is present in all the creation
Five evils lust, anger, greed, attachment and egotistical pride
Gurbani the divine Words of the Guru that lead the soul to God
Gurmantar the mantra from the Guru, "Vaheguru"
Jap to repeat the Gurmantar in a loving way
Mantra a word or words that are repeated as part of a discipline
Maya the temporary, illusionary world
Rajo a part of Maya that makes us desire fame, wealth and recognition
Sadh Sangat the congregation of saintly people
Sato a part of Maya that makes us virtuous but with "spiritual desires"
Sikh literally means "learner", one who learns from the True Guru
Tamo a part of Maya that makes us behave from our animal or base instincts
Turiya the fourth state where we rise above Maya

# SHARE CHARITY

SHARE Charity is a UK based charity that has been running since 2007. SHARE stands for Sikh History And Religious Education and it aims to provide resources at a global level to teach about the Sikh faith. One of the worldwide projects that the charity is known for is the Sikhi To The Max software which was the first search engine available to search Gurbani in a practical way. It is used worldwide and set the standard for searching Gurbani using first letters and other innovative features.

We also have many other initiatives, such as the publishing of books for all ages, producing digital media and videos, digital artwork in the form of infographics to teach about the faith and we have recently started to create podcasts. The Sikhi Enlightenment Course is a very practical one-day workshop on Sikh spirituality that has been well received in many countries. We have also developed various mobile applications to learn about the faith and Gurbani, including Sikhi To The Max for both Apple and Android.

The charity has raised money for and organised eye camps for the underprivileged in India, We have partnered with Clinical Care Pharmacy to raise funds for charitable initiatives too. All orders for medicine through the pharmacy help to support our projects because all profits from the medicines distributed are to given to SHARE charity.

You can visit our website and our social media sites using the addresses below:

www.sharecharityuk.com

https://www.youtube.com/sharecharityuk

https://www.instagram.com/sharecharityuk

https://www.facebook.com/sharecharityuk

https://soundcloud.com/sharecharityuk


Available Apps:

1) Sikhi To the Max

2) Supersant

3) Learn Gurmukhi

4) Simran Reminder

# INDEX

Why Am I Here?: The soul, the Guru and the path is an excellent resource for anyone wanting to learn about Sikhi. Practical advice backed by English quotations from the Guru's words. Contents include Ego, Gratitude, Karma, Mental Health, Virtues, and much more. Anyone with the slightest understanding of Sikhi to those who have been practicing the faith for years will benefit from reading this book.
- Amardeep Singh

Fascinating insight in to this beautiful way of life. A very highly recommended spiritually guided masterpiece for those seeking enlightenment.
- Mo Majid

★ ★ ★ ★ ★

This book is a gem. Not just for Sikhs but for anyone trying to answer that universal soul seeking question on why are we here? What are we here to do? It takes this big question and distils it in an easy to understand way. A must read for all!
- R Kaur

★ ★ ★ ★ ★

Fantastic book. Captures the essence of Sikhi and Spirituality in 15 easy to read chapters. Highly recommended.
- J Singh

Why Am I Here For Kids is a new sticker book for kids to learn about Sikhi spirituality in a fun and loving way! Meet the Sangat family, the wicked witch Maya, and the five niggly monsters.

Watch out, watch out, wherever you are! She peeks through the window and sneaks near the door. She throws her terrible, colourful blanket onto the world! She lives in her dusty dungeon with cauldrons and cobwebs. Watch out for her cackle and the evil grin because Maaya, the wicked witch is out and about! What will happen when she sends her five niggly monsters to the Sangat's family's home? Why Am I Here is a fun, interactive story sticker book that explores the power of Naam and Gurbani. It's full to the brim of interesting characters and witty humour! It's a book that keeps you on your toes in its page-turning adventure! With brilliant, bright illustrations that will capture your child's imagination, this sticker book is one you won't put down! Don't forget to complete the challenges and receive a certificate at the end of your journey!

Get your copy today along with other exciting resources by visiting the sharecharityuk.com website.

Please visit sharecharityuk.com/give/
and help us deliver more projects by
donating